The British Association for
Shooting and Conservation

HANDBOOK OF SHOOTING
An introduction to the
sporting shotgun

The British Association for
Shooting and Conservation

HANDBOOK OF SHOOTING
An introduction to the sporting shotgun

Quiller

CONTRIBUTORS

Tom Blades
Graham Downing
John Harradine
Bill Harriman
Peter Marshall
Jane Matthews
Jeffrey Olstead
Tim Russell
Jamie Stewart

Design

Alistair Kennedy
Sarah East

ILLUSTRATIONS

Ian Danby
Hayden Davies
Rob Douglas
Nick Ridley
Lee Selvester
Jeffrey Olstead
Charles Sainsbury-Plaice

Acknowledgments

Members and staff of BASC past and present who have all contributed over the years.

First published in the UK in 1983
This sixth edition published 2010
by Quiller, an imprint of Quiller Publishing Ltd

British Library Cataloguing-in-Publication Data
A catalogue record for this book
is available from the British Library

ISBN 978 1 84689 059 8

Printed in China.

Quiller

An imprint of Quiller Publishing Ltd
Wykey House, Wykey, Shrewsbury, SY4 1JA
Tel: 01939 261616 Fax: 01939 261606
E-mail: info@quillerbooks.com
Website: www.countrybooksdirect.com

CONTENTS

9 Foreword by HRH The Prince Philip, Duke of Edinburgh

10 Introduction to the principles of live quarry shooting

12 Shotguns and cartridges

30 Shotgun safety

41 The law relating to shooting

51 Behaviour in the field

55 Quarry identification

95 Rough shooting

101 Driven game shooting

107 Wildfowling

117 The role of gundogs

125 Gamekeeping

129 Care of shot game

131 Shooting and conservation

136 Appendices

141 Index

If you are thinking of taking up game shooting, or know of someone who might be interested, this is the book for you. It contains everything you should know about the sport, so that you can participate without fear of doing anything wrong or embarrassing.

It may be 26 years since this book was first published, but the basic principles of the shooting sports have not changed. Guns are lethal weapons, so that the most important consideration is safety. The quarry is live game, therefore the second priority is to make certain that there is no unnecessary suffering. Consequently, the chapters on behaviour in the field, shotgun safety and the law are extremely important.

All this, together with much useful information and guidance, has been collected together in this book. I believe that it should be compulsory reading for all beginners, and I am sure that it will be interesting for shooters.

HRH The Prince Philip, Duke of Edinburgh
Patron of the British Association for
Shooting and Conservation

INTRODUCTION TO THE PRINCIPLES OF LIVE QUARRY SHOOTING

The purpose of this book is to explain the principles of using a shotgun to shoot live birds and mammals. Although it will be of particular value to those taking the Principles of Live Quarry Shooting (PLQS) course it is intended as a general introduction for any newcomer to sporting shooting. There are more detailed works on all aspects of the sport and you should certainly read as much as you can about it, but there is no substitute for practical experience; lessons at a shooting school or from a qualified coach are essential if you are to get the most enjoyment out of shooting sports.

That enjoyment is hugely increased by the context in which shooting takes place – good company, beautiful countryside and, if the shoot is well managed, an abundance of wildlife. Shooting puts far more back into the countryside than it takes out; if you take up the sport you also shoulder this responsibility.

Responsible shooting is the wise use of a sustainable resource, and that is why a considerable portion of this book is devoted to conservation. It is no accident that the representative body for live quarry shooting is called the British Association for Shooting and Conservation (BASC).

Traditionally, BASC has placed a great deal of emphasis on education and training. Some time ago the education sub-committee produced a set of codes of practice for the sport to guide those seeking basic information. This was done because we believe that we have a duty to encourage high standards of safety, sportsmanship and courtesy among those who enjoy the legitimate sport of shooting.

Following the codes of practice we established the proficiency award scheme (PAS) which was a way for those who shoot to improve their knowledge. The PAS has since evolved into the Level 2 Certificate in the Principles of Live Quarry Shooting, which is no longer offered by BASC but by the National Proficiency Tests Council (NPTC) which ensures the award remains current and available to all over 16s.

NPTC is the largest nationally recognised awarding body in the land-based sector. It works closely with Lantra, the sector skills council for land-based training and education, to ensure that qualifications are current and reflect the industry's needs. NPTC is an accredited awarding body with the Qualifications and Curriculum Authority (QCA) and part of the City & Guilds Group.

The certificates (mostly at Level 2) provide practical skills assessments in a wide range of land-based tasks. The PLQS qualification is aimed at candidates who wish to develop a basic understanding of traditional country shooting, game and wildlife identification, and the use of gundogs. It is suitable for people who may:
- have no previous experience of shooting
- be required to have an understanding of shooting as part of their employment
- be considering taking up shooting as a recreation
- be interested in game conservation or habitat management
- be seeking a career in land management.

Its aim is to provide an accredited qualification that is available to anybody wishing to develop an understanding of live quarry shooting with a shotgun.

The primary purpose of this *Handbook of Shooting - The Sporting Shotgun* is to teach shotgun safety, sportsmanship, including respect for the quarry, the law and courtesy.

It will help those who shoot to derive far greater enjoyment in the knowledge that they are conducting themselves to high standards of behaviour in the field.

Much of the criticism levelled against shooting sports is a direct result of either misunderstanding or of bad behaviour witnessed in the field. The rights and privileges of sportsmen to continue to enjoy their sport, and the satisfaction of helping to conserve the countryside and wildlife, depend very much on the behaviour of all shooting people. They will be judged by their attitude and behaviour.

The social structure of the shooting community has altered considerably in the last few years. There are many now who wish to take up the sport, or indeed who have entered it but have no real knowledge of shooting and the traditions of the countryside, or of the quarry species they pursue, and their management needs.

PLQS has therefore been introduced to give everyone who shoots a practical means of attaining the BASC ideal – 'that all who shoot lawfully in the UK conduct themselves according to the highest standards of safety, sportsmanship and courtesy, with full respect for their quarry and a practical interest in wildlife conservation and the well-being of the countryside'.

To learn more about the Level 2 Principles of Live Quarry Shooting visit the NPTC website at www.nptc.org.uk.

1 – SHOTGUNS AND CARTRIDGES

You may have inherited a gun, been given one or, more probably, bought it yourself for the particular kind of shooting that you're interested in. But however you acquired the gun it is important to understand how it is made, how it works, its care and use, so that, together with suitable cartridges, it can be used effectively and responsibly in the shooting field.

SHOTGUNS

Definition of a shotgun

The Firearms Act 1968 defines a shotgun as: 'A smooth-bore gun, not being an air rifle or a revolver gun, with a barrel not less than 24 inches and with a bore not exceeding 2 inches. It must either have no magazine or a non-detachable magazine incapable of holding more than two cartridges.'

This definition allows for various types of shotgun, incorporating different features.

Construction of shotguns

Modern shotgun barrels are made of steel and are either drilled or drawn out of a solid cylindrical piece of steel.

In the past shotgun barrels were made by twisting thin strands of iron and steel together and welding them into a tube. Barrels made in this manner are known as Damascus barrels and they may be found on a small number of guns still in use. Many will not have been proved (see page 32) for modern nitro powders, and can only be safely used with black powder.

Types and features of shotguns

Double-barrel guns

The standard game gun used to be a double-barrel hammerless ejector 12-bore shotgun of drop-down opening style. The configuration of the barrels was side-by-side. It had a top lever to open the gun and barrels between 25in and 30in in length, with either a sidelock or boxlock action, double triggers and an automatic safety catch. It had fairly open choke and was chambered for 65mm (2½ in) or 70mm (2¾ in) cartridges. It had a stock, fore-end and rib.

However, shooters today increasingly use the over-under shotgun, which is broadly similar but the barrels are placed one above the other. Guns of this type are very popular for rough shooting and wildfowling, increasingly are used for game shooting and are universally used for clay target shooting.

Standard O/U game gun

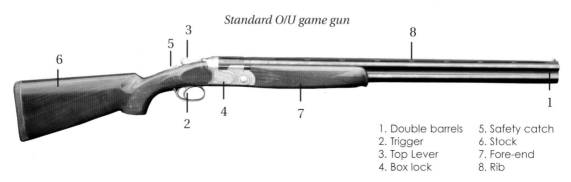

1. Double barrels
2. Trigger
3. Top Lever
4. Box lock
5. Safety catch
6. Stock
7. Fore-end
8. Rib

Single-barrel guns

The most common alternative to the double-barrel shotgun is the single-barrel gun and this can take a number of forms depending on how it works. A common form is a single shotgun, similar to the side-by-side already described but with only one barrel. Some single-barrelled guns, however, are capable of firing more than one shot.

Single-barrelled pump-action and semi-automatic shotguns may be operated on one of three principles: manual, gas pressure or recoil. There are also bolt-action shotguns.

Pump-action shotguns have a manually-operated sliding fore-end which, when pulled back and pushed forward, ejects the fired cartridge and brings the next cartridge from the magazine into the chamber, ready for firing.

Gas pressure-operated self-loaders use gas from the fired cartridge to operate a mechanism in the breech that ejects the empty cartridge and inserts a fresh one into the chamber.

Recoil-operated self-loaders work by a process of barrel or chamber recoil generated by the firing of a cartridge. The operating principle is the same as for the manually-operated pump-action shotgun except that the 'pump' occurs automatically on recoil.

Note: Single-barrelled pump-action and semi-automatic or self-loading shotguns may be possessed on a shotgun certificate provided that they have a non-detachable magazine incapable of holding more than two cartridges.

Bolt-action single-barrel guns require a single cartridge to be inserted into a receiver which is exposed when the bolt is drawn back. Pushing the bolt handle forward and locking it engages the cartridge in the chamber; reversing this action removes the empty case.

Occasionally guns are seen which have three barrels, the third usually being placed centrally below the other two side-by-side barrels. The third barrel is normally rifled (i.e. internally grooved) for firing bullets and is intended for use against large ground game. These guns are much more common in continental Europe than in the UK (where a firearms certificate would be required).

Pump-action shotgun

Bolt-action shotgun

Rib

On a side-by-side shotgun the rib is used to join the barrels to each other and as a sighting device along which to line-up the barrels with the target.

On over-under shotguns, the rib is used solely as a sighting aid.

Side-by-side
shotgun

Over-under
shotgun with rib

**Boxlock and
sidelock action**

Boxlock and sidelock are alternative actions used in shotguns. The action is, in simplified terms, the firing mechanism.

Boxlocks are cheaper to manufacture than sidelocks because they are simpler in design and have fewer components.

Sidelock actions are more complex than boxlocks, but give easier access to the mechanism for cleaning. They generally give a better balance and are found on more expensive guns.

Hammerless

Hammerless refers to the absence of visible, exterior hammers (which shotguns originally had). Hammerless guns were first patented in 1863. Hammer guns are still in use, but a number of older ones may not have been proved for use with modern cartridges. Modern shotguns are hammerless.

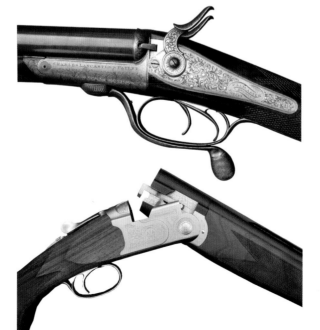

*Hammer gun with
under lever*

Hammerless gun

Opening of guns

Drop-down action refers to the manner in which the shotgun is opened for the purposes of loading and reloading. Side-by-side and over-under guns have drop-down actions but single-barrel guns, which are semi-automatic, pump or bolt-action, reload mechanically or manually without the need to open the gun.

A distinct advantage of the drop-down style is that it allows the user to check that the barrels are clear of obstruction before loading when, for instance, snow or mud may have entered the barrel. You can also check after noticing any abnormal noise or recoil on firing.

The standard drop-down action shotgun has stood the test of time and is universally accepted whereas pump-action and self-loading shotguns are not always

Drop-down action of an over-under shotgun

welcomed on shoots. This is largely because it is not possible to see immediately whether these guns are empty, as it is with a drop-down action when the gun is 'broken', or open. However, there is nothing inherently dangerous about pump-action or self-loading shotguns.

Ejector

The ejector throws out, or ejects, fired cartridge cases when the gun is opened; unfired cartridges are not ejected. Modern shotguns typically have ejectors.

A non-ejector shotgun does not throw out spent cartridges, but will lift an empty case slightly - thus enabling the user to grip the cartridge and manually extract it.

Semi-automatic and pump-action shotguns eject the spent case as part of the sequence of firing and bringing up the next cartridge into the chamber.

Stock

The stock houses part of the action, and allows you to mount and fire the gun. It is important that the stock is fitted to ensure that when the gun is brought up to the shoulder it is correctly aligned with the shooter's master eye.

Cast of a stock

The term 'cast' refers to the degree to which the stock is bent to the right or left in relation to the line of the barrel(s) in order to bring the barrel(s) in line with the shooter's master eye.

Cast is measured at the butt and is termed 'cast off' if it is to the right and 'cast on' if it is to the left as you look down the gun from the butt end. Shotgun stocks, made either traditionally of walnut or, increasingly, plastic, can be bent or cast to suit the shooter's requirements.

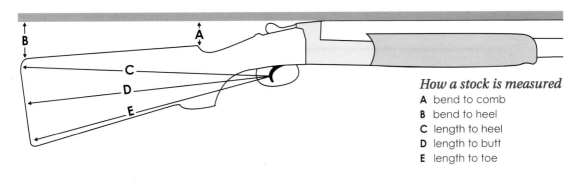

How a stock is measured
A bend to comb
B bend to heel
C length to heel
D length to butt
E length to toe

Shapes of shotgun stock

Game guns conventionally have a straight stock, but some people prefer a pistol or semi-pistol grip, which they find easier to handle. It is entirely a matter of personal choice.

Straight

Semi-pistol

Full-pistol

Top lever

The top lever is the mechanism by which most shotguns are opened. Occasionally you may encounter shotguns with side-levers or under-levers. Non drop-down guns do not require opening levers.

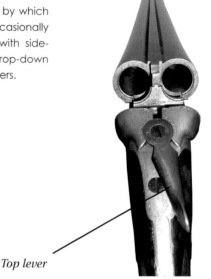

Top lever

Triggers

Double-barrel shotguns may be fitted with double triggers, one for each barrel, or with a single trigger which may be selective or non-selective.

On a side-by-side with double triggers, usually the front trigger fires the right-hand barrel and the rear trigger fires the left-hand barrel. On a left-hand gun the triggers may be the other way round.

On an over-under shotgun with double triggers, the front trigger usually fires the bottom barrel and the rear trigger fires the top barrel. However, many over-under shotguns have a single trigger.

Double-barrel shotguns can be fitted with a single trigger which may or may not be selective. If the single trigger is selective, the shooter can choose which barrel they fire first, thus allowing for a choice of choke. The selecting device is normally incorporated into the safety catch.

Safety catch – automatic and manual

The safety catch locks the triggers so that they cannot be pulled. However, this does not immobilise the firing mechanism and it is possible for a gun to be discharged by a knock or a jar, or even a hard pull on the trigger.

Safety catches may be automatic, i.e. returning to 'safe' when the gun is opened, or manual, i.e. not returning to 'safe' as part of the process of opening the gun. With manual safety catches, you must yourself return the gun to 'safe' after reloading. Many semi-automatic or pump-action shotguns have a sliding-button safety catch on the trigger guard which is usually non-automatic.

Take extra care with safety catches which are non-automatic.

Do not rely on any safety catch to make a shotgun safe.

With a loaded gun there is always the risk of an unintended discharge. Treat all closed guns as loaded.

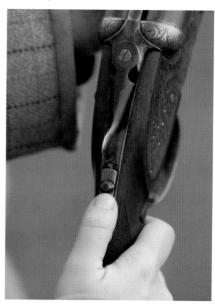

Safety catch

Breech

The breech of a shotgun is the near end of the barrel. It consists of the chamber which contains the cartridge and the breech block which seals the end of the barrel preventing the escape of high-pressure super-heated gases. In a pump-action or semi-automatic shotgun it is the breech block itself which runs forwards as the action cycles.

The fences are the bulbous bits that project to the rear of this. In a bolt action gun, this is the front face of the bolt.

Chamber

The chamber of a shotgun is that part of the barrel nearest to the action into which the cartridge is inserted. Chambers are of different lengths. Most 12-bore shotguns are chambered for 65mm (2½ in), 67.5mm or 70mm (2¾ in) or 76mm (3 in) cartridges. Some now have 89mm (3½ in) chambers for big, steel shot wildfowling cartridges.

It is dangerous to fire any cartridge which is longer than the chamber is designed to take.

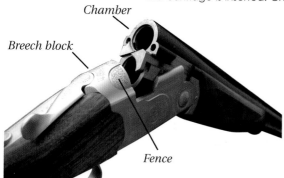

Chamber

Breech block

Fence

Fore-end

The fore-end locks the barrels into position and provides the forward hand grip for the shooter. It should not be too smooth and it should be large enough to prevent the fingers of the forward hand encroaching upon the rib and thus obstructing the line of sight.

Fore-end over-under

Fore-end side-by-side

Bore

Shotguns are classified by the size of the bore, which is the internal diameter of the barrel. Historically, the bore size or gauge (American) was measured by the number of spherical balls of pure lead, each exactly fitting the interior diameter of the barrel, required to make up one pound in weight.

How a bore used to be measured: 12-bore

Therefore, because a 20-bore required 20 such lead spheres and a 12-bore required 12, the 20-bore is of a smaller bore than the 12-bore. Today the measurement is usually made with a bore gauge.

The .410 shotgun, however, is commonly found, but, historically, its bore was described by the nominal internal diameter of the barrel in inches, i.e. 0.41in. It is equivalent to a 67-bore gun.

Comparative cartridge sizes: (L to R) 4-bore, 8-bore, 10-bore, 12-bore, 28-bore

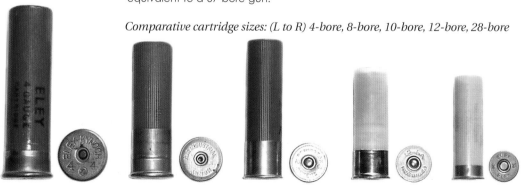

Shotguns may be typically encountered in (nominally) 4, 8, 10, 12, 16, 20 and 28 bore, and .410, although other obscure bores do exist.

Today's game gun is usually a 12-bore, which is suitable for most types of sporting shotgun shooting, provided the appropriate cartridge is used. However, relatively light 20-bores are becoming increasingly popular for game shooting.

The 16-bore is suitable for most forms of inland shooting, but is more common in continental Europe than in the UK.

The 28-bore is often used to introduce young people to shooting. The .410 is unsuitable for sporting shooting except in skilled hands. However, it is a useful shotgun for pest control at relatively short range.

The 10-bore is widely used for coastal wildfowling, particularly goose shooting, and has increased in popularity since the restrictions on lead shot. This is because it fires a larger load of steel shot compared with the 12-bore. The 4 and 8-bore are more rarely encountered today, but popular among some traditional wildfowlers.

Each of these different bores of shotgun has its strengths and weaknesses and needs to be used accordingly, bearing in mind the type of shooting and the ability of the shooter.

Choke

When a cartridge is fired the pellets, after travelling up the barrel, leave the muzzle and begin to spread. The further they travel, the wider they spread, and eventually they will spread so much that not enough pellets will hit the target. Most shotgun barrels therefore incorporate 'choke' which is a constriction at the muzzle end that is designed to reduce the spread of the shot as it travels down range.

There are five, traditional, degrees of choke. Starting with the tightest degree of restriction they are:

A degree of choke at the muzzle

UK	*Standard US*
1. Full choke	1. Full
2. Three-quarter choke	2. Improved modified
3. Half choke	3. Modified
4. Quarter choke	4. Improved cylinder
5. One-eighth choke (often referred to as improved cylinder)	5. Skeet

Conventionally, choke is measured as the reduction in bore diameter, in thousandths of an inch, relative to the standard un-choked bore diameter for each type of gun. In a 12-bore, for example, full choke is around 40'thou' less than the standard 0.729in bore diameter, while quarter choke is around 10'thou' less. Note that all these labels and measurements are nominal and can vary from gun-maker to gun-maker.

If there is no restriction at the muzzle the bore is described as true cylinder.

Fixed-choke and multi-choke

Guns are made either with specified degrees of choke already built into their barrel ends or with a set of removable 'multi-chokes'. In a fixed-choke gun, choke can be removed by a gunsmith, thereby opening up the bore at the muzzle, but it is very difficult – and expensive – to replace it.

In over-under shotguns the lower barrel, as it is usually fired first, typically has a more open choke than the top barrel. For the same reason, in a side-by-side game gun, the right barrel usually has more open choke than the left barrel.

Many guns nowadays are multi-chokes and have interchangeable choke tubes that vary in their degree of constriction. The shooter selects a choke tube which is screwed into the muzzle of the gun, enabling them to vary the pellet pattern density. The tubes must be seated carefully, and frequently checked and cleaned, otherwise the barrels may become damaged.

Interchangeable barrel chokes

Effect of choke

The two-dimensional distribution of pellets in a circle, traditionally 30inch diameter, at a given range, recorded on a pattern plate or large sheet of paper, is known as the 'pattern'. The tightest pattern, i.e. the greatest number of pellets in that circle, is usually, but not always, produced by full choke. The most open pattern, i.e. that in which the pellets are most spread out, is generally produced by the true cylinder. But it should be noted that the density of pellets produced by each degree of choke can be highly variable from cartridge to cartridge and not always possible to predict.

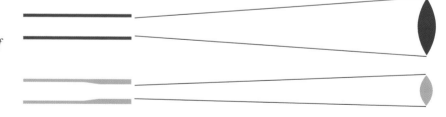

Comparison of effect of open (top) and tight chokes (not to scale)

A tightly-choked gun may be more suitable where shots are regularly taken at longer ranges, but it will require greater accuracy on the part of the shooter (because the pattern is smaller). However, this does not mean that a tighter choke necessarily increases the range of shooting – it primarily increases the likelihood of striking the target with more pellets. The degree of choke used is largely dependent upon personal choice, but most shooters use relatively open chokes rather than tight ones, often preferring improved cylinder in the first barrel and quarter or half choke in the second. Ability to hit your target consistently, though, is much more important than worrying about the degree of choke in your barrels.

Remember – a tight choke should not be used to increase the range of a shotgun.

Gun fit

You will have gathered from the previous sections that there are various options when you buy a gun – length of barrel, degree of choke and suchlike – that you can choose. But unless you are wealthy enough to have a gun built specially for you, your gun will come with standard, off-the-peg dimensions, which is fine if you are an off-the-peg person. Unfortunately nobody is, and unless the gun is fitted to the person using it, they will never shoot well.

The gun should be of reasonable fit in stock length; a rough guide to fit is a three-fingers gap between the thumb of the trigger hand and the nose when the gun is mounted. The stock should also be of the correct height; if the comb is too low your head may lift off the stock and you'll shoot below the target; if the comb is too high you will shoot over the target.

Seemingly small discrepancies in the height or angle of the stock can make a crucial difference to the accuracy of shooting so it is important to get your gun fitted by a qualified gunsmith. He can make adjustments to the stock to ensure that you can mount the gun properly, and that it points where you want it to – that it is aligned with your master eye.

Master eye

Most people have a dominant eye which, put simply, is the one that the brain prefers. When the brain receives images from both eyes it processes the information from one of them first, and that's your master eye.

When aligning a distant object, the target, with a closer one, the barrels, the master eye's picture will be the one used by the brain – as long as both eyes remain open. It's obvious, therefore, that to point a gun accurately at a target you must mount the gun in the shoulder directly under the eye doing the work. This is particularly important for shotgun shooting where you generally need to have both eyes open to pick up fast and unpredictable targets.

Eye dominance has little to do with quality of vision. If you wear glasses your master eye may still be the weaker of the two, and just to make it more confusing, eye dominance may change with age.

If possible, then, establish which is your master eye and shoot from that shoulder. This should not be a problem for novice shooters but more experienced shooters, those whose eye dominance has changed, or those who simply find it too difficult to adjust to right or left-handedness, may need to close the master eye as the gun is mounted. This will allow the eye which is over the rib to establish the correct sight picture.

To determine which is your master eye follow this simple procedure:
1. Hold a pencil upright at arm's length in your left hand.
2. Look through both eyes and line the pencil point up with an object on the other side of the room.
3. Close your right eye. If the pencil and the object are no longer in line, you have a right master eye.
4. Close your left eye. The object will still be in line with the pencil.
5. If, when you closed your right eye, the object and the pencil were still in line, then you have a left master eye.

CARE AND MAINTENANCE OF A SHOTGUN

There are three good reasons for maintaining a shotgun in good working order:

- To ensure that it remains in a safe condition
- To reduce the risk of mechanical malfunction at any time
- To preserve an asset which may appreciate if looked after

A shotgun should be cleaned after each use.

Phosphor-bronze brush

There are a number of methods and materials which may be used to clean a shotgun, but the following will ensure that it is kept clean and rust-free.

The recommended cleaning kit consists of:

- Cleaning rod
- Tissue paper, kitchen paper or rolled-up newspaper
- Proprietary brand of gun oil or cleaner, either as liquid or aerosol
- Phosphor-bronze brush
- Lambswool mop
- Pipe-cleaners
- Soft cloth/rag

To clean the stock

The following is based on the assumption that the shotgun has been used on a wet day.

First detach the barrels from the stock.

Hold the stock firmly and give it a good shake. On a wet day water which has penetrated the mechanism should be shaken out.

Remove all visible water from the exterior of the stock.

Remove any mud, dirt or blood from the stock and clean any chequering, possibly with a soft toothbrush, to remove any dirt.

Rub over the metal parts with a lightly-oiled rag.

To clean the fore-end

Use the same method as for the stock.

Oiling with a lambswool mop

To clean the barrels

Remove all visible water from the barrels and run a piece of tissue, as tightly as possible, along the guttering beside the rib.

Fold or roll up the newspaper or tissue and push it through the barrels with the cleaning rod – the tissue should be as tight as possible – from the chamber to the muzzle. This will remove the worst of any powder or other fouling on the inside of the barrels and will enable you to keep your cleaning materials relatively clean.

Cleaning the barrel

The next stage is to attach the phosphor-bronze brush to the cleaning rod and with short, sharp, backward-and-forward movements work the brush all the way along the inside of the barrels to remove all traces of lead and other residues.

The barrels, when held up to a light and looked through, should be bright with no tell-tale streaks visible. To complete this stage of the cleaning, put a thin smear of oil along the inside of the barrels using the lambswool mop or spray. Remember that the oil must be removed before the gun is used again, as too much left inside can create a dangerous hindrance to the next fired cartridge.

Raise the extractors and with a pipe cleaner, or a piece of cloth over a small stick, clean out any remaining powder residues.

Below are some general but important points:

General maintenance

Do not over-oil a shotgun. The oil may dry out and solidify, resulting in a 'gumming-up' of the moving parts. The parts which require the merest drop of oil from time to time are those which receive the greatest friction. On a sidelock gun it is a straightforward process to remove the locks to enable drying and cleaning of the action. With a boxlock it involves the removal of the bottom plate (positioned just forward of the trigger guard).

Whenever attempting to remove any screw, it is essential that the screwdriver is of an accurate fit to avoid damaging the screw head.

If your gun has received an extensive soaking, place it in a warm, dry area with the barrels positioned to allow any water in the gutters alongside the rib to run off. Do not place the stock too near a direct source of heat, or in too warm a place, as the wood may warp or split. Re-examine the gun after a few hours to make doubly sure that no rust has begun to develop.

When cleaning your gun, examine it for faults or damage.

When putting your gun into its case or slip, hold the barrels with a cloth to avoid leaving finger marks which could form the basis for rust.

If you are not using your gun for a while, examine it from time to time to ensure that no rust is building up while it is in storage.

Shotguns should be sent to a competent gunsmith for a clean and overhaul every year. Do this well before the season opens in order to avoid a last-minute panic.

SHOTGUN CARTRIDGES

Understanding how a cartridge works is just as important as knowing how the shotgun works. For successful shooting it is the appropriate combination of gun and cartridge together that greatly influences the outcome of each shot.

Note that production of a shotgun certificate is normally necessary to purchase ammunition.

As the 12-bore is the most widely-used shotgun, all references in this section, unless stated otherwise, will refer to 12-bore game cartridges and their variations.

Cartridge components

1. Case
2. Wad (fibre)
3. Powder
4. Crimp closure
5. Shot
6. Primer

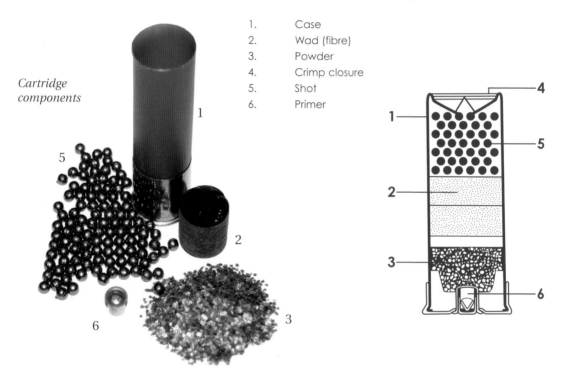

Care of cartridges

Store cartridges at normal room temperature, out of the sun and away from sources of heat and damp, and great cold. Poor storage conditions can affect the performance of cartridges.

Cartridge length

Cartridges, for safety reasons, should not be used if they are longer than the chamber length of the gun. Thus a gun with 65mm (2¹/₂in) chambers may take a 65mm cartridge but not a 70mm (2³/₄in) one. A gun with 70mm chambers may safely take a 65mm, 67.5mm and a 70mm cartridge.

Cartridge case

The case is the outer shell of the cartridge. It is both a container for the remaining components of the cartridge and it has to seal the chamber so that all the gas pressure created by firing is directed along the barrel and is not allowed to escape.

It is preferable that the case is waterproof and for this reason most cartridges have plastic cases. Cartridges with paper cases are occasionally used. The main disadvantage with paper cases is that they are not waterproof and may swell if they become damp. Paper cases may also split if they become abnormally dry. However, an advantage of paper-cased cartridges is that spent cases are biodegradable, whereas most plastic cases are not.

Crimp closure

Crimp closure refers to the manner in which the cartridge is sealed. The case is made sufficiently long to allow the top to be turned in towards the centre in a star pattern. In the past, cartridges were manufactured with a roll closure, in which the end of the cartridge was pressed over a card disc which retained the shot.

Powder

The original propellant in shotguns was gunpowder – known as black powder. It was a mechanical mixture of potassium nitrate, sulphur and charcoal. It produced a considerable amount of white smoke and caused serious fouling to the barrels. However, with a slower burn than its successors, it did produce a less fierce recoil.

During the late nineteenth century nitro-cellulose based propellants were introduced. They quickly superseded black powder, though it may still be used in some elderly, large-bore wildfowling pieces and by muzzle-loading firearms enthusiasts.

All modern cartridges are loaded with nitro powders which offer consistent performance, are almost smokeless, and being cleaner significantly reduce the risk of corrosion in gun barrels. They also produce much greater pressures when fired so all guns that fire modern cartridges must be proofed for nitro powders. It is dangerous to fire a nitro cartridge in a gun which was only designed for black powder.

Primers

The propellant powder is ignited by a primer. This is a small cap in the base of the cartridge which explodes when struck by the gun's firing pin. A common cause of misfires is the failure of a firing pin to hit the primer centrally or hard enough.

Wad

The wad is the component of the cartridge which is situated between the powder and the shot. When the powder burns, the wad acts as a piston with the expanding gases behind it, forcing the shot ahead of it along and out of the barrel. Wads may be made either of plastic or fibre. Plastic wads normally have a shot cup to protect the shot from abrasion as it travels along the barrel, which might otherwise affect the shot pattern. However, plastic wads are a source of litter. Fibre wads are biodegradable and for that reason are preferred on many shoots and most shooting grounds.

Note: steel shot cartridges normally require plastic wads to prevent pellets from causing excessive wear to barrel walls. Biodegradable wads are slowly becoming available for steel shot.

Shot

A shotgun normally fires a charge of shot, comprising a large number of roughly spherical pieces of metal or metal-based material, usually lead but increasingly nowadays substitute materials. In a typical game cartridge there may be some 270 - 350 pellets. The number varies considerably according to the type of cartridge and shot size.

Shot sizes are identified by letters (for the larger sizes) and numbers (for the smaller sizes). Shot sizes in the UK are (nominally) as follows:

Size	Diameter in mm	Diameter in inches
LG	9.1	.36
SG	8.4	.33
Spec.SG	7.6	.30
SSG	6.8	.27
AAA	5.2	.20
BB	4.1	.16
1	3.6	.14
3	3.3	.13
4	3.1	.12
5	2.8	.11
6	2.6	.10
7	2.4	.095
7.5	2.3	.09
8	2.2	.085
9	2.0	.08

Other countries, including the USA, use different scales of sizes. If in doubt refer to the diameter in millimetres.

The total weight of shot in cartridge is the 'load' and this varies according to the type of shooting. A 24g ($^7/_8$oz) load in a 12-bore gun, for example, is widely used as a light cartridge for clay target shooting. A 32g ($1^1/_8$oz) load is popular for game shooting. A 36g ($1^1/_4$oz) load may be used as a heavier load for some wildfowling, in suitably-chambered guns.

There are many other load weights for other bores of gun, ranging from 8g ($^5/_{16}$oz) in the .410 to 64g ($2^1/_4$oz) or more in an 8-bore or 4-bore. The larger the shot size, the greater will be the potential striking energy of each pellet but there will be fewer pellets in the shot pattern, in a given load weight. The smaller the shot size, with the same load weight, the denser the pattern of shot will be on the target, but each pellet has less, and perhaps insufficent striking energy.

Very occasionally, a suitable shotgun may be used to fire a single ball or a rifled slug for killing large animals, such as wild boar. A firearms certificate is required to possess and use such ammunition.

Non-lead shot

Non-lead shot is required in certain situations for shooting waterfowl and waders, and for shooting over wetlands. In England and Wales lead shot cannot be used for shooting any waterfowl anywhere; it is also banned on or over the foreshore and on or over designated sites of special scientific interest important for waterfowl. In Scotland and Northern Ireland the law prohibits the use of lead shot on or over all wetlands.

Steel, bismuth, tungsten-based and certain other shot materials are used in place of lead. Their characteristics are different from lead and different loads, shot sizes, components and shooting techniques may be needed. Extra care is needed with the hard shot types like steel, and International Proof Commission (CIP) regulations guide their use in different types of gun.

Shot sizes

Traditionally, different pellet sizes in lead shot have been favoured for different types of shooting, such as:

Geese - BB/1/3   **Grouse** - 6/7   **Hare** - 4/5

Mallard - 4/5/6   **Partridge** - 6/7   **Rabbit** - 5/6

Teal - 6/7   **Pheasant** - 5/6/7   **Grey squirrel** - 7

Snipe - 8   **Woodcock** - 7   **Pigeon** - 6/7

Recent research, however, may result in recommended shot sizes changing, generally towards larger pellets than were used in the past. Furthermore, each non-lead type has different ballistic characteristics. This means that pellet sizes may need to change for these materials to achieve pattern density and striking energy levels sufficient to ensure consistently clean kills. In particular, where the material is less dense than lead, and so has less kinetic energy, it is necessary to use a larger size shot – for example, if steel then at least two sizes larger (i.e. for lead no.6 use steel no.4 or larger); if bismuth then at least one size larger (no.3 or larger in place of lead no.4).

While the traditional game load has long been 30g or 32g (1¹⁄₁₆ oz and 1⅛ oz) of no.6 shot nowadays game shooters are using more no.5 or larger shot.

Remember – a heavy load does not necessarily increase the effective range of a shotgun.

Shotgun range

The range of a shotgun is not simply the maximum range at which it is capable of killing a particular quarry – it is the range at which, with an appropriate cartridge, it will consistently do so. A gun and cartridge combination which only occasionally kills, after hitting a vital spot by luck, will inevitably result in an unacceptable level of wounding and loss of shot game.

The maximum effective range of your shotgun in relation to a given kind of quarry is the greatest range at which you are reasonably certain that a clean kill will be made by a truly-aimed shot. Consistently hitting and killing your target, with the appropriate gun/cartridge combination, is the most important factor in successful shooting.

In effect, this means that with an appropriate 12-bore cartridge the maximum effective range could be some 32-37m (35-40yd), but it may well be less than this, depending on your ability to shoot well. If you cannot hit and kill your target consistently at, say, 32m (35yd), you should not attempt to shoot at that range. As your shooting skill improves, through practising on clays, for example, you can extend your range.

Smaller-bore guns generally have a correspondingly lower maximum effective range, not least because the smaller load fired by the gun typically has fewer pellets to strike the target.

There are at present 18 codes of practice, produced by BASC and others, to help you shoot safely and responsibly. You will find a full list, with contact details, in Appendix 2 (p 137).

Shotgun patterning

The 'appropriate gun/cartridge combination', to which we have already referred, is the combination of load weight (i.e. number of pellets) and pellet size which is expected to achieve a clean kill, on each type of quarry, at the range at which you can consistently hit your target.

Each shooter should know how their gun 'patterns' with each chosen cartridge i.e. whether the spread of pellets on the pattern plate is dense enough to ensure a clean kill of the quarry. You cannot rely on books or published charts. The only way to be sure is to test cartridges of each type through your chosen gun/choke combination because every cartridge and every cartridge/choke combination is likely to pattern differently.

The process is to fire, separately, at least five test cartridges at the pattern plate or paper, at the range of your shooting accuracy; place the 30in circle over the densest part of each pattern; and count the number of pellet strikes inside. The average pellet count of the test cartridge then reveals its suitability for the intended type of shooting. If the count is too low then the cartridge, choke or range can be changed until it is adequate.

For example, American scientific research indicates the following minimum pellet count (of the correct size pellets) for different types of quarry:

Geese – 65   **Pheasant –** 100
Large duck – 90   **Partridge –** 140
Medium duck – 120   **Pigeon –** 140
Small duck – 140

After shooting at a pattern plate count the number of pellets in the 30in circle

2 – *SHOTGUN SAFETY*

HANDLING A SHOTGUN

Always treat any gun as loaded and therefore potentially dangerous

Checking that a gun is empty

Even when you have emptied the gun or checked that it is unloaded *(left)*, safety precautions must not be disregarded.

It is not sufficient simply to assume that a shotgun is unloaded when you first handle it; it must become an automatic reaction to check that it is unloaded by opening it, if the action is of the drop-down variety, or by examining the breech and chamber, if it is a semi-automatic or a pump-action gun.

Accidents have occurred when a loaded gun was assumed to be empty. You must always check.

Always pass a shotgun to someone stock first with the breech open and empty, and demonstrate clearly that the gun is not loaded

Always ensure that the barrels are not pointed at anything which you do not intend to shoot

This is a sound principle which should be practised whether the gun is loaded or not. If the gun is loaded always point it in a safe direction, ideally at the ground or the sky.

Always carry a gun open and empty when in company

A gun with a conventional drop-down action is best carried over the forearm.

Always take special care with pump-action and semi-automatic guns

It is not as easy for someone else to see that a pump-action or semi-automatic shotgun is unloaded as it is with a gun that has a conventional drop-down action. When in company carry such guns with the slide or action open and with the muzzle pointing upwards. Auto-safety flags which can be inserted into the chamber are another good way of demonstrating that these types of guns are unloaded and safe.

With pump-action or self-loading shotguns always take special care to ensure there is no obstruction in the barrel.

Remember that there are particular problems relating to hammer guns

Always carry hammer guns in the uncocked position, with the hammers down. On the immediate expectation of a shot, cock the hammers whilst ensuring that the barrels are pointing straight upwards, placing the finger around the outside of the trigger guard and the thumb in the crutch of the hammer.

Always open the gun before uncocking the hammers. If you cock the hammers in the expectation of a shot but do not fire one or both of them, **do not uncock the hammer(s) onto a loaded chamber.**

If the right hammer in the cocked position obstructs the top lever, consult a gunsmith.

Always ensure that any shotgun you intend to use is in a safe and sound condition

Make certain that the internal mechanism is in a proper state of repair and adjustment.

You must be able to recognise the following potential problems which can occur with shotguns:

Denting and/or bulging of the barrel

A dent causes a constriction in the barrel which will result in excessive pressure and wear in the barrel (and may result in a serious accident). A bulge is a weakening of the structure of the barrel.

Corrosion

Rust and corrosion are signs of poor maintenance. They may result in the weakening of the barrels and action, and in malfunction.

Pitting of the barrels

Pitting can occur both inside and outside the barrels and result in a weakening of the barrel strength. It is caused by poor care and maintenance.

Raised ribs

Raised ribs (if caused by rusting) will involve a weakening of the barrel wall and almost certainly a weakening of the barrel structure.

Damaged or cracked stocks

A cracked stock may break as a result of recoil and is a potential hazard to the shooter and anyone nearby.

Loose action

The action should be correctly aligned to the barrels so there is no movement when the gun is closed, ensuring that gas pressure is not allowed to escape when the gun is fired.

Trigger pulls

Trigger pulls must be correctly adjusted. If they are too light to be felt by a cold or gloved finger, the gun may be discharged unintentionally.

Always have your gun regularly serviced by a competent gunsmith

Any faults should be rectified immediately, and a gun should be checked every year by a competent gunsmith.

Important information will have been marked on your gun during its manufacture and testing

The name of the manufacturer, serial number, chamber length or proof pressure, bore size and proof marks may be found engraved or stamped onto the barrels, top rib, action flats, action body or lock plates.

Always ensure that you understand the proof markings on any shotgun you use

Proof marks demonstrate that the gun has been tested by a proof house. The law relating to the proving of guns is to be found in the UK Gun Barrel Proof Acts and in various Rules of Proof. While the acts and rules are complex, the reason you need to understand the proof markings on a gun is straightforward; you will not unwittingly use a dangerous load.

Proof marks

The proof mark will show the pressure at which the gun has been tested ('proved'). This pressure, in turn, sets the limit on the cartridges which can be safely fired in that gun. Typically a cartridge generating a chamber pressure up to some 30% less than the proof pressure is safe to use. Never use a cartridge exceeding that chamber pressure.

Always follow the guidance given by cartridge makers on their boxes as to in which gun the cartridges are safe to use.

Always ensure that any gun you intend to use is safe and in proof for the cartridges you intend to use

If any doubt exists, the gun should be examined by a gunsmith because:

- *An unproved gun may be in a dangerous condition and should not be used. It is a hazard not only to the user but also to any other person nearby.*

- *It is illegal to sell or offer for sale an unproved gun. The maximum penalty is £5,000 for each offence.*

Always remember that a shotgun may be out of proof

Even if a gun bears valid proof marks, excessive wear or damage may mean that safety tolerances have been reduced below acceptable limits. If a gun appears worn or damaged, it must be checked by a gunsmith.

Always leave a shotgun in such a way that it cannot be knocked or fall over

The barrels of a shotgun are made of steel, but they can easily be damaged by a knock or fall. If you put an unloaded shotgun down, pay particular attention to where it is placed, avoiding all hazards.

Never put a loaded shotgun down

Never allow unsupervised children to handle guns or cartridges

Children are by nature inquisitive and want to find out about things; guns and cartridges are no exception, so do not leave them unattended and ensure that they are always out of reach of children.

Introduce youngsters to supervised and correct gun handling at an appropriate age and in accordance with the law.

SHOTGUN SAFETY IN THE HOME

Never load a shotgun indoors

This rule is absolute. There is no reason whatsoever for loading a shotgun indoors.

Always store your shotgun and cartridges securely

The law requires that guns which are not in use must be stored securely, so far as is reasonably practicable, to prevent access by unauthorised persons. In most cases this will be achieved by keeping them in a locked gun cabinet, but other devices such as security cables or clamps may also be effective. Do not disclose the location of the security keys to anyone who is not authorised to access the guns.

Always keep your shotguns and cartridges in separate, safe places, locked away, out of sight

Cartridges should be secured against casual access, and kept away from extremes of heat or humidity.

Clean your gun before putting it away

Remove the slip or cover, clean the gun and oil it to reduce condensation and corrosion before putting it in the cabinet or other secure place.

Always keep a record of shotgun serial numbers or, if there is no number, of any other distinguishing marks. In the event of loss or theft of your shotgun this will enable you to give a full and accurate description to the police. A photograph is ideal.

SHOTGUN SAFETY WHILE TRAVELLING

Never travel with a loaded shotgun

Before entering a vehicle check that your shotgun is unloaded. When anyone enters a vehicle with a shotgun which is not in a case or cover, or which you cannot see is empty, satisfy yourself that the gun is unloaded.

Always when travelling carry your shotgun in a case or protective cover

This will protect the gun against damage and prevent public concern and the attention of police.

Shotgun being carried in a protective cover

Always lock unattended vehicles

Whenever leaving a vehicle which contains guns or cartridges, even if only for a brief period, make certain that the vehicle is securely locked. Remove a component part from the gun such as a fore-end and carry it with you where possible.

Always when travelling to or from a shoot or a clay ground ensure that your shotgun and cartridges are stored and secured out of sight in the vehicle

SHOTGUN SAFETY IN THE FIELD

A gun which is not in immediate use should be unloaded and in a slip

Carry a gun which is in a slip with the muzzles pointing down. This prevents it from falling out if the fastening fails or comes undone.

Removing a gun from its slip

1. Unfasten the slip.

2. Open the gun, or check a safety flag is inserted in the breech, and check that it is unloaded before the barrels emerge.

3. Fully withdraw the gun from the slip.

Putting a gun into its slip

1. Insert the barrels of the open gun into the slip, checking that it is unloaded.

2. Close the gun (or open the breech and insert a safety flag if it is a semi-auto or a pump-action).

3. Fully insert it into the slip.

4. Fasten the slip.

How to close a shotgun safely

Always lift the stock to the barrels, not the barrels to the stock.

Always carry a shotgun so that it cannot point at anyone – always be 'muzzle aware'

Never load a shotgun until you are about to start shooting

Always load a shotgun by placing the cartridge in the chamber and raising the stock to the barrels

Always make sure the barrels are pointing in a safe direction when reloading

Always keep your fingers well clear of the triggers except when taking a shot

How to carry a gun over the crook of the elbow

Never attempt to shoot unless you are steady on your feet

Taking a shot whilst unsteady could result in the shooter losing balance at the moment of firing with potentially lethal consequences.

Never attach a dog's lead to yourself, while shooting

If the dog is unsteady enough to require to be tied up, it may decide to move as you are about to fire, thus causing you to overbalance. Either secure the dog elsewhere or train it to be steady.

SAFETY CATCHES

Always have the safety catch on 'safe' until the moment before you wish to fire

The safety catch should be released only as the gun is raised to the shoulder.

Take special care if a gun does not have an automatic safety catch

Most guns have a safety catch which engages automatically when the gun is opened, but some guns have a manual safety catch which must be put to the 'safe' position by the shooter after the gun is loaded.

Remember that the safety catch is merely a mechanical device which prevents the trigger from being pulled – the gun may still be loaded and the action cocked, and if the safety catch malfunctions the gun may discharge. A gun is not safe unless it is unloaded.

Always be sure of what you are shooting

Positively identify your target before raising your shotgun to the shooting position. If in doubt, do not shoot.

Always be aware of what is beyond your target

Do not fire if you cannot see where the shot will go: for example do not shoot at bushes or a hedge. Do not fire where ricochets could occur, for example at rocks, water or frozen ground.

Always be certain of your 'safe arc of fire'

The safe arc of fire, as the name suggests, is the arc through which you can swing a gun and take a shot without endangering neighbouring guns or other people. It involves the position of others, the topography of the ground, the risk of ricochet and the fall of spent shot, which can travel over 350 metres, depending on wind and shot size.

Standing in a line of guns you will have a relatively narrow forward arc of fire. To swing through the line is absolutely forbidden, though you may, depending on shoot rules, and if it is safe, be able to take a shot behind. If you are shooting alone or are standing at the end of a shooting line, it may be safe to swing through a wider arc. But again this will depend on where other people are positioned and the lie of the land.

Safe arc of fire

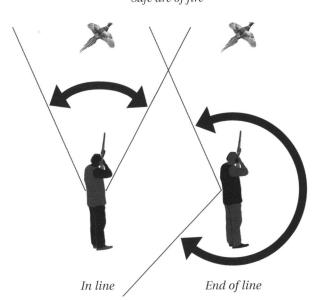

In line   *End of line*

Always be aware of the possibility, and the consequences, of a misfire

This is when a cartridge refuses to fire. You should also beware of a hangfire; in this situation the cartridge does fire, but only after a delay, which could be as long as 30 seconds. If there is a misfire, point the barrels safely at the ground and wait at least 30 seconds before opening the gun and removing the cartridge.

If there is an uncharacteristic noise or recoil from a particular shot, make certain that you look down the barrel in a safe fashion before taking another shot, to determine that there is no obstruction. Check that the barrels are not cracked or damaged.

Always unload your shotgun before crossing an obstacle or negotiating difficult terrain

Negotiating an obstacle in company:

1. Both shooters open their shotguns and remove cartridges.

2. The first shooter passes their gun, open and stock first, to their companion.

3. Having crossed the obstacle, the first shooter takes both guns from their companion.

4. The second shooter clears the obstacle.

5. They take back their gun and check for blockage or damage before reloading.

Negotiating an obstacle alone:

1. Open your shotgun and remove cartridges.

2. Place the gun on the near side of the obstacle in such a way that it cannot fall over or be damaged.

3. Clear the obstacle.

4. Pick the gun up and check for blockage or damage immediately or certainly before reloading.

These procedures apply to fences, gates and similar obstacles.

Always look through your barrels to check whenever an obstruction could have entered and remove anything immediately

Never mix cartridges for shotguns of different bores

If, for example, a 20-bore cartridge is placed into the chamber of a 12-bore, it will enter the barrel far enough to allow a 12-bore cartridge to be placed in the chamber above it and the gun to be closed and fired. The result could well be serious damage to the gun and injury to the user or observers.

Severely damaged shotgun as a result of cartridge mixing

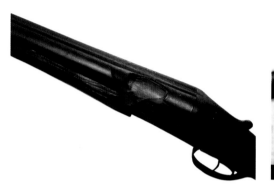

Never shoot without public liability insurance

Membership of BASC automatically provides the following insurance package:

£10 million legal liability cover (for all shooting categories)

£10 million employer liability cover (for all shooting categories)

£10 million product liability cover (for all shooting categories)

Safety is a level of consciousness – not a fortunate series of events

Safety is the responsibility of everyone – including you!

3 – THE LAW RELATING TO SHOOTING

SHOTGUN CERTIFICATES

How to obtain a shotgun certificate

In order to possess a shotgun in Great Britain (England, Wales and Scotland) it is necessary, subject to certain exemptions, to hold a shotgun certificate (see page 42).

Obtain an application form from the police or downloaded from the internet. Complete it and have it countersigned as described on the form, then send it with the appropriate fee and four passport-style photographs to the firearms licensing department at your police headquarters.

Conditions of issue

Shotgun certificates are valid for five years from the date of issue. Most police forces will issue reminders to shotgun certificate holders shortly before the expiry date of the certificate. **However, it is the shotgun certificate holder's own responsibility to renew their certificate.**

A shotgun certificate is issued subject to the following conditions:

• The holder must, on receipt of the certificate, sign it in ink with their usual signature.

• The holder must immediately inform the chief officer of the police force by whom it was granted of the theft, loss or destruction in Great Britain of his certificate or of the theft, loss, deactivation or destruction of any shotgun to which it relates.

• The holder must inform the police of any change in their permanent address without undue delay.

• The holder must ensure that shotguns to which their certificate relates are stored securely so as to prevent, so far as is reasonably practicable, access to the guns by an unauthorised person. They must also ensure safe custody of the guns while they are in use or in transit.

The police may refuse to issue a shotgun certificate if they are satisfied that an applicant does not have a good reason for possessing a gun, or cannot be permitted to possess a shotgun without danger to public safety or the peace.

Prohibited persons

A person who has been subject to a term of imprisonment of three or more years is prohibited from possessing a shotgun.

A person who has been subject to a term of imprisonment of up to three years is prohibited from possessing a shotgun for five years from the date of release.

Transfer of shotguns

When a shotgun is transferred to anyone other than a registered firearms dealer each party to the transaction must notify their own chief officer of police within seven days by secure post. 'Transfer' includes selling, giving as a gift, hiring or a loan of more than 72 hours.

Exemptions from the requirement to hold a shotgun certificate

Certain categories of persons do not require a shotgun certificate. This is what the law says:

- A person carrying a firearm (including shotgun) or ammunition belonging to another person holding a certificate under the Firearms Act 1968 may, without himself holding such a certificate, have in his possession that firearm or ammunition under instruction from that other person and for the use of that other person for sporting purposes only. This may be interpreted to include, for example, a loader

- A person may, without holding a shotgun certificate, borrow a shotgun from the occupier of private premises (including private land) and use it on those premises in the occupier's presence

- A person may, without holding a shotgun certificate, use a shotgun at a time and place approved for shooting at artificial targets by the chief officer of the police force for the area in which that place is situated. This will include an authorised shooting school or clay pigeon shooting ground

- Visitors to Great Britain who wish to use, possess, purchase or acquire shotguns and ammunition may do so if they hold a visitor's shotgun permit. Application for such permits must be made on the visitor's behalf by a 'sponsor' who is resident in Great Britain, to the chief officer of police for the area in which the sponsoring person resides

- A person does not commit an offence in Great Britain if he has in his possession, purchases, or acquires a shotgun if he holds a firearm certificate issued in Northern Ireland authorising him to possess a shotgun (see below)

- A person does not commit an offence if he holds a temporary permit issued by the police under Section 7 of the Firearms Act 1968.

European Firearms Pass

The European Firearms Pass (EFP) enables EU citizens to travel between member states with firearms and ammunition for sporting or competition purposes. UK certificate holders may obtain an EFP from their firearms licensing department free of charge. The EFP is valid for the life of the holder's shotgun certificate and is renewable.

Residents of other EU member states visiting Great Britain with their shotguns require an EFP issued by the authorities in their country of residence in addition to a UK visitor's shotgun permit.

Northern Ireland

Possession of shotguns, firearms and air weapons in Northern Ireland is covered by a single firearm certificate issued by the Police Service of Northern Ireland (PSNI). Possession of a Northern Ireland firearm certificate exempts the holder from the requirement to hold a shotgun certificate in England, Scotland and Wales.

Visitors to Northern Ireland who are resident in Great Britain and who hold a shotgun certificate must obtain a certificate of approval from the PSNI before travelling with their gun. They must produce to the authorities on arrival their British shotgun certificate and the NI certificate of approval.

POSSESSION OF SHOTGUNS BY YOUNG PEOPLE

There is no lower age limit for the grant of a shotgun certificate, but there are limitations on the age at which young people may possess or purchase shotguns and ammunition.

Under 15

It is an offence to make a gift of a shotgun or ammunition to a person under 15 years of age.

A person under 15 may not have an assembled shotgun with them except:
(i) when they are under the direct supervision of someone of or over 21, in which case they may use the shotgun, providing they have a valid shotgun certificate, under that person's instructions;
(ii) when the shotgun is in a securely fastened gun cover so that it cannot be fired.

Aged 15-17

A person between 15 and 17 years of age may be given or lent a shotgun and ammunition, but they may not buy or hire them.

Upon reaching the age of 15, a person may use a shotgun without supervision providing they hold a valid shotgun certificate.

17 and over

Upon reaching the age of 17 a person may buy or hire a shotgun providing they hold a valid shotgun certificate, and they may buy ammunition.

Young people in Northern Ireland

The chief constable may grant a firearms certificate to a person between 16 and 18 years of age for a shotgun, but only if it is to be used for pest control or the protection of livestock on agricultural land occupied by the young person or on which they work and also reside.

The chief constable may grant a firearms certificate to a person between 16 and 18 years of age for a shotgun for sporting purposes provided they are under the direct supervision of a person who has attained the age of 21 years and has held a firearms certificate for that type of firearm for at least three years.

POLICE POWERS

When out shooting, it is advisable to carry your shotgun certificate with you. A constable may demand from any person whom he believes to be in possession of a shotgun, the production of his shotgun certificate.

If a person upon whom a demand is made fails to produce the certificate or to permit the constable to read it, or to show that he is entitled by virtue of the Firearms Act to have the shotgun in his possession without holding a certificate, the constable may seize and retain the shotgun and may require the person to give him his name and address.

Appeals against refusal to grant or renew a certificate

If the police refuse to grant or renew a shotgun certificate, or if they revoke an existing certificate, you may appeal to the Crown Court, or the Sheriff Court in Scotland, by giving notice, within 21 days of receiving the notice of refusal or revocation, to the clerk of the court and the chief officer of the police force for the area.

In Northern Ireland you may appeal to the Secretary of State.

SHOTGUNS IN PUBLIC PLACES

Carrying a firearm in a public place

A person commits an offence if, without lawful authority or reasonable excuse (the proof of which lies on him), he has with him in a public place a loaded shotgun. 'Loaded' means having cartridges in the chamber, or the magazine if the gun has one.

'Public place' includes any highway or any other premises or place to which the public has access at the time in question.

Trespassing with a firearm

A person commits an offence if, while he has a firearm (including a shotgun) with him, he enters or is on any land as a trespasser and without reasonable excuse (the proof of which lies on him). Land includes that covered by water.

A person commits an offence if, while he has a firearm (including a shotgun) with him, he enters or is in any building or part of a building as a trespasser and without reasonable excuse (the proof of which lies on him).

Shooting on or near a highway

It is an offence to shoot, without lawful authority or reasonable excuse, within 50 feet (15.25m) of the centre of a highway if in consequence someone on the highway is injured, interrupted or endangered.

Footpaths and bridleways

A person having the right to shoot on land over which a right of way (footpath or bridleway) passes has lawful authority and reasonable excuse to shoot on or near the footpath or bridleway, but must do so responsibly and with regard for other people.

SHOOTING GAME IN ENGLAND, WALES AND SCOTLAND

Game may only be shot at certain times of the year – the open seasons. 'Game' includes pheasant, partridge, red grouse, black grouse, ptarmigan and hare. The seasons in England, Wales and Scotland are:

Pheasant:	1 October – 1 February
Partridge:	1 September – 1 February
Red grouse/ptarmigan:	12 August – 10 December
Black grouse:	20 August – 10 December
Hare:	No close season except on moorland and unenclosed land. See BASC website for details.

All dates are inclusive. It is illegal to shoot any species out of season.

In England and Wales it is illegal to shoot game on Sundays, Christmas Day or at night, and although not illegal in Scotland it is not customary to do so. Night is taken to mean the period from one hour after sunset to one hour before sunrise local time.

THE USE OF SHOTGUNS IN RELATION TO THE WILDLIFE AND COUNTRYSIDE ACT 1981

Protection of wild birds in England, Wales and Scotland

The Wildlife and Countryside Act 1981, as amended, protects all wild birds (except those covered by the Game Acts), their nests and eggs, subject to clearly defined exceptions. These exceptions provide for open seasons during which certain species may be shot, and they lift restrictions on shooting certain 'pest' species throughout the year.

Remember that all species are protected. Some receive special protection all year or during the close season. Penalties for killing or harming protected species are severe.

Quarry species

The species which may be shot during the open season:

Coot	**Pintail**
Gadwall	**Plover**, *golden*
Goldeneye	**Pochard**
Goose, *Canada*	**Shoveler**
Goose, *greylag*	**Snipe**, *common*
Goose, *pink-footed*	**Teal**
Goose, *white-fronted (England and Wales only)*	**Tufted duck**
	Wigeon
Mallard	**Woodcock**
Moorhen	

Pest species and general licences

General licences allow authorised persons to kill those species which are commonly regarded as 'pests' for specific purposes such as preventing damage to crops, property, public health, or for conservation or air safety. The licences are issued annually by the devolved governments and individual shooters do not need to apply for one. However, they must comply with the terms and conditions of the specific licences, and species and conditions differ between countries with each administration issuing its own licences. The species concerned are:

Crow *(carrion and hooded)*
Dove, *collared*
Goose, *Canada (England only)*
Gull, *great black-backed*
Gull, *lesser black-backed*
Gull, *herring*
Jackdaw
Jay *(Not on all licences in Scotland)*
Magpie
Pigeon, *feral*
Sparrow, *house (Not in England)*
Starling *(Not in England)*
Woodpigeon

Authorised persons

Under the Wildlife and Countryside Act, an 'authorised person' means:

(a) the owner or occupier, or a person authorised by the owner or occupier, of the land on which the action authorised is taken;

(b) any person authorised in writing by the local authority for the area within which the action authorised is taken;

(c) any person authorised in writing by the relevant government conservation body, a water authority, or local fisheries committee constituted under the Sea Fisheries Regulations Act 1966; but with the proviso that the authorisation of any person for the purpose of this definition shall not confer any right of entry upon any land.

Racing pigeons

Racing pigeons may not be shot at any time.

SHOOTING WILD BIRDS IN ENGLAND, WALES AND SCOTLAND

Seasons in England, Wales and Scotland

The seasons during which certain birds may be killed or taken are as follows:

Woodcock *(England & Wales)*	1 October – 31 January
Woodcock *(Scotland)*	1 September – 31 January
Common snipe	12 August – 31 January
Ducks and geese *(above the high water mark of ordinary spring tides)*	1 September – 31 January
Ducks and geese *(below the high water mark - see pages 107-8 for definitions)*	1 September – 20 February
Coot, moorhen, golden plover	1 September – 31 January

All dates are inclusive.

It is illegal to shoot these species on Christmas Day in England, Scotland and Wales, and on Sundays in Scotland and certain counties and county boroughs in England and Wales (these are listed on page 110).

Periods of special protection

Under exceptional circumstances, for example prolonged severe weather or serious pollution, the Department for Environment, Food and Rural Affairs (Defra), or a devolved government, may make an order protecting wild birds, including waterfowl and waders. This will be done in accordance with criteria and procedures previously agreed by government, shooting and conservation organisations. Before making such an order, the relevant secretary of state will consult a representative of those who shoot the species of birds to be protected by the order (i.e. BASC).

Typically, if severe weather lasts 13 days, a statutory suspension order comes into effect on the 15th day. Earlier in that period BASC may call for extra voluntary restraint in shooting where the conditions merit it.

Non-lead shot

To minimise the poisoning of waterfowl from ingested lead shot there are restrictions on its use. In England and Wales lead shot may not be used below the high water mark of ordinary spring tides, on or over many wetland sites of special scientific interest (SSSIs) important for waterfowl, or for shooting waterfowl, wildfowl, coots and moorhens anywhere. In Scotland and Northern Ireland lead shot may not be used for shooting on or over wetlands.

Prohibited methods

The following methods (relating to the use of shotguns) of killing or taking wild birds are prohibited:

- Using any self-loading shotgun which has a magazine capable of holding more than two cartridges.

- Using any shotgun of which the barrel has an internal diameter at the muzzle of more than 44mm (1³/₄ inches).

- The use of any device for illuminating a target.

- The use of any form of artificial lighting or any mirror or other dazzling device.

- The use as a decoy of any sound recording, or any live bird or animal which is tethered, or which is secured by means of braces or other similar appliances, or which is blind, maimed or injured.

- The use of mechanically propelled vehicles in immediate pursuit of a wild bird for the purpose of killing or taking that bird.

Sale of dead wild birds

Generally the sale of dead wild birds is prohibited, but the sale of the following is allowed at all times:

Pigeon, *feral*
Woodpigeon

Sale of the following dead wild birds is allowed during the period
1 September – 28 February only:

Coot	**Snipe,** *common*
Mallard	**Teal**
Pintail	**Tufted duck**
Plover, *golden*	**Wigeon**
Pochard	**Woodcock**
Shoveler	

Shot woodpigeon may be sold at all times of the year

PROTECTION OF WILD ANIMALS IN ENGLAND, WALES AND SCOTLAND

The Wildlife and Countryside Act 1981, as amended, provides protection to wild animals and lists in Schedule 5 those species which are specially protected. These species are unlikely to be encountered while shooting, except for the red squirrel, bats and the badger. Confusingly a number of these animals, which already enjoy total protection, are then listed on a separate schedule – Schedule 6 – as 'species which may not be killed or taken by certain methods'. The effect of this is to imply that the 'certain methods' are legal for all the unprotected species. Listed below are the methods which are banned for all species and then the methods which are illegal for the animals on Schedule 6, but may be used to control the unprotected species.

Prohibited methods for killing or taking any wild animal

It is illegal to use certain methods for killing or taking any wild animal. The sporting shotgun shooter should be aware that he is guilty of an offence if he:
- Uses for the purpose of killing or taking any wild animal any self-locking snare, any bow or crossbow or any explosive other than ammunition for a firearm (including shotgun).

- Uses as a decoy, for the purpose of killing or taking any wild animal, any live mammal or bird.

However a general licence (this means you do not need to apply for it specifically but must comply with its terms and conditions) allows some birds to be kept in certain cage traps for pest control purposes. The issue of the licence is reviewed annually.

Prohibited methods for killing or taking Schedule 6 animals

Additionally, animals which appear in Schedule 6 may not be killed or taken by the following methods:
- Any semi-automatic weapon.

- Any device for illuminating a target or sighting device for night shooting.

- Any form of artificial light or any mirror or other dazzling device.

It is also an offence to:
- Use as a decoy, for the purpose of killing or taking any such wild animal, any sound recording.

- Use any mechanically propelled vehicle in immediate pursuit of any such wild animal for the purpose of driving, killing or taking that animal.

The above methods are by implication permitted for the purpose of taking or killing those animals which do not appear in Schedules 5 or 6.

SHOOTING GAME AND WILD BIRDS IN NORTHERN IRELAND

All birds, their eggs and nests are protected at all times by the Wildlife (Northern Ireland) Order 1985. The Order, however, makes provision for certain species to be killed or taken at certain times by authorised persons.

Birds which may be killed or taken outside the close season:

Curlew	**Pochard**
Gadwall	**Scaup**
Goldeneye	**Shoveler**
Goose, *Canada*	**Snipe,** *common*
Goose, *greylag*	**Snipe,** *jack*
Goose, *pink-footed*	**Teal**
Mallard	**Tufted duck**
Pintail	**Wigeon**
Plover, *golden*	

Birds which may be killed or taken by authorised persons at all times under the terms and conditions of a general licence:

Crow, *carrion*   **Pigeon,** *feral*

Crow, *hooded*   **Rook**

Gull, *great black-backed*   **Sparrow,** *house*

Gull, *herring*   **Starling**

Gull, *lesser black-backed*

Jackdaw

Magpie

Birds which may be sold dead at all times:

Woodpigeon

i.e. the sale of any other dead wild bird is prohibited at all times.

Game birds

The Wildlife (Northern Ireland) Order 1985 defines gamebirds as pheasant, partridge (chukar partridge and red-legged partridge), woodcock, common and jack snipe, and red grouse.

Shooting seasons in Northern Ireland

Grouse	12 August – 30 November
Pheasants	1 October – 31 January
Wild ducks, geese and waders*	1 September – 31 January
Woodcock	1 October – 31 January
Snipe	1 September – 31 January
Hares	12 August – 31 January
Partridge	1 September – 31 January

All dates are inclusive.

*Refers only to those birds which appear in Schedule 2 Part I of the Wildlife (Northern Ireland) Order 1985 (see previous page).

Non-lead shot

It is illegal to use lead shot on or over wetlands in Northern Ireland.

THE GAME ACTS

Game licences

Game licences in England and Wales were scrapped in 2007. They are still required by law in Scotland and Northern Ireland, although in Scotland they are expected to be abolished in 2010. Licences should be acquired from your local post office or through BASC Scotland or BASC Northern Ireland. Game in Scotland is generally defined as hare, pheasant, partridge, red grouse, black grouse and rabbits in some circumstances. A game licence is also required if stalking deer on unenclosed ground in Scotland.

Hares

However you do not require a game licence to shoot hares, provided that you are shooting on land where you are the owner (having the right to kill game), occupier or a person duly authorised in writing under the provisions of either the Hares Act 1848 or the Ground Game Act 1880.

Only one person can be so authorised and must be one of the following:
1. A member of the occupier's household resident on the land;
2. A person in the occupier's ordinary service on the land;
3. A person genuinely employed for reward to kill and take hares and rabbits on the land.

Night shooting

'Night' is taken to mean the period from one hour after sunset to one hour before sunrise.

England and Wales

• Game may not be shot at night
• Rabbits may be shot at night by the landowner or by persons authorised by him
• Hares may be shot at night by authorised persons.

Scotland

• Game may not be shot at night
• Rabbits and hares may be shot at night by authorised persons.

Northern Ireland

It is illegal to shoot wild birds at night, but not to lamp foxes and other pests.

The law relating to land ownership

There is very little free shooting in the UK. Shooting rights will almost always be held by the landowner or shooting tenant and under a measure of control.

If you shoot anywhere without permission, you lay yourself open to prosecution for armed trespass or trespass in pursuit of game (poaching).

According to the circumstances, you can be charged with one or both of these offences.

Always ensure that you are authorised to shoot where you intend to go.

4 – BEHAVIOUR IN THE FIELD

The following is a general code of conduct regarding behaviour when out shooting. More guidance on behaviour when game shooting, rough shooting and wildfowling, is given in the appropriate sections.

Always remember that it is the sportsman's responsibility to know the laws relating to his sport

You must know and obey the laws relating to the sport, particularly those concerning shotguns and your quarry (see Chapters 1 and 3).

Always ensure that you are authorised to shoot where you intend to go

It is advisable to have written permission to shoot. You must know precisely where the shoot boundaries are located; an annotated map may be helpful.

Advise the owner and/or the tenant in good time if you want to go shooting

Check that it is convenient for you to go shooting at the time you intend to go. Check for restrictions which might affect your sport.

Always ensure that your shotgun certificate is signed and valid

Carry your shotgun certificate or a photocopy of it whenever you go out shooting.

Always respect the owner's property

Respect crops, livestock, property and fences; damage to property may result in a loss of shooting rights.

Open gates rather than climb them. Close gates after you if they were closed initially – you may cut stock off from water by closing a gate intentionally left open. Climb a secured gate at the hinged end.

Do not break fences, rails or damage hedges.

Do not walk in standing corn; seek the farmer's guidance in respect of other growing crops.

Always observe the BASC Shotgun Safety Code (see Appendix 2)

This is outlined in Chapter 2 and you should be thoroughly conversant with it.

Know and respect public rights of way

Know the location of any public rights of way in the area and take care near them not to frighten or endanger their users. Remember that the public may not always stay on rights of way.

Always have a dog with you and keep it under control

Do not shoot without the use of a trained gundog to retrieve shot game.

Do not let your dog disturb livestock. Sheep in lamb can be harmed if made to run; a dog need not chase sheep to cause them to panic. It is an offence for a dog to worry livestock on agricultural ground or be at large (that is, not on a lead or otherwise under close control) in a field or enclosure in which there are sheep.

Always wear suitable and sensible clothing and footwear to suit your surroundings

Make contingency plans for wet and cold weather and carry appropriate clothing.

Always remember that others will judge the sport by your behaviour and that of your companions

If you observe others behaving in a manner likely to bring the sport into disrepute, politely but firmly bring their responsibility to the sport as a whole to their attention.

Always remember your responsibility to help safeguard your quarry and its habitat for future generations

Know the quarry species and their respective seasons, respect them and help to look after their habitats.

Always avoid causing unnecessary disturbance to other users or occupiers of the countryside

Avoid shooting close to other properties and at night if the noise may be a nuisance to others.

Do not shoot towards or frighten livestock.

Do not allow shot to fall onto another property

It is discourteous and a civil offence (trespass) to allow shot to travel over a boundary onto another property without due permission.

Always ensure that your shooting is as good as possible

You will improve your shooting by practice on clay targets. Recommended methods of shooting a moving target are given in Appendix 4.

Never let excitement cloud your judgement

Concentration and attention to safety are vital at all times.

Never let alchohol cloud your judgement

Like drinking and driving, shooting and drinking do not mix; you are just as likely to injure yourself as someone else and even a little alcohol can affect your judgement. Be particularly careful on a formal shoot where shooting may continue after lunch. An unsafe or irresponsible Gun will probably be asked to leave the shoot and certainly will never be invited back.

Always shoot within your own range

Remember that it is unacceptable to shoot at any quarry which is beyond the range of your capabilities.

Allow flushed quarry to gain reasonable distance (say, 15yd) before shooting, though, to prevent it from being too damaged for eating. Pest and predator shooting may be excepted in the case of close shots, but out-of-range shooting at pests or predators is also inexcusable.

Do not shoot a bird or animal just because it is within your range

Although it may be in your range, it may provide a more sporting shot for somebody else.

Always 'mark' shot quarry carefully

Watch each shot bird or animal carefully to make sure you know where it will be retrieved. If it is wounded ensure that it is picked up without delay and dispatched immediately.

Every effort should be made to locate, pick up and humanely despatch wounded quarry as soon as possible after shooting it. Do not move on or try to shoot another bird or animal before you have retrieved the first one.

Always dispatch wounded quarry as humanely and as quickly as possible

A sharp knock on the head with a suitably heavy stick or 'priest' (pictured left) is most effective for birds.

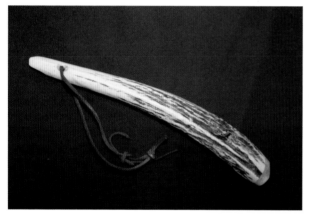

Hares and rabbits can be killed by holding them by the head between the first and second fingers, with the first finger extended under the creature's chin, and quickly jerking the animal downwards, so dislocating the neck.

Always observe the BASC code of practice for safe gun-handling when dispatching wounded quarry.

If quarry is shot and falls or runs over the boundary, you must seek permission of the landowner to retrieve it

Your gun must be left (safely) behind unless the landowner has given you permission to shoot over his land. Otherwise, you could face possible proceedings for armed trespass. It is also a trespass (civil) to send a dog onto another's land without permission even if it is to retrieve a shot animal.

Always take your quarry from the game bag as soon as possible at the end of the shooting day

Store it in a cool, fly-proof place. Do not waste it.

Always remember that the enjoyment of sport is not reflected by the size of the bag

Do not shoot excessive numbers. A viable stock should be left on the ground at the end of the season wherever possible. Shooting for crop protection, though, may be an exception.

Never leave litter

Take all your litter home with you. This includes empty cartridge cases.

Whenever possible pick up litter left by someone else. Litter can be a hazard to livestock. Leave the countryside as you find it for others to enjoy.

5 – QUARRY IDENTIFICATION

The sportsman's responsibility is to ensure that he positively identifies his quarry before taking a shot

It is essential that you should be able to distinguish rapidly between quarry and non-quarry species in the field. The primary aim of this guide is to help you learn the techniques of species identification, with particular reference to the main quarry species, but the principles established apply equally to other birds and animals. Through practising field identification at every opportunity you will not only become competent at recognising the species you seek, but will also benefit from the ability to identify non-quarry animals.

It is important to have access to field guides and texts to help you learn the characteristic field marks of wildlife. It is equally important for you to appreciate that no amount of theory can substitute for experience in the field.

Species identification is a craft, the skills for which are acquired through field experience

This chapter is simply an introductory guide, covering only those species commonly pursued with a shotgun. You should take every opportunity to practise quarry identification under a wide range of field conditions, and use a more comprehensive field guide. The experience gained through attempting to identify all species encountered, regardless of their quarry status or time of year, will enhance your enjoyment of the countryside and eliminate the risks of shooting at non-quarry species. Comprehensive field guides are readily available both as books, which can be carried in a pocket for field use, or on DVD which shows the animal in its natural habitat and which, for birds, has the advantage of showing flight patterns and distinctive calls.

HOW TO IDENTIFY QUARRY SPECIES

The aim of this guide is to establish the basic principles for recognising quarry species

Species identification is achieved through learning the key field-marks and behaviour which distinguish particular groups and species from one another, enabling the bird or animal under observation to be positively identified.

The features which provide the most useful clues to quarry identification are the animal's size, shape, markings, colour, general behaviour and distribution in both space and time. Positive species identification usually results from a combination of the various diagnostic features.

See Appendix 5 for recommended field guides

Size and shape It is helpful to compare with a familiar species in the same group and also to note any distinctive features of the animal's shape which permit identification in silhouette, including, in the case of birds, those features which are readily seen in flight.

Colour and pattern Note any unique colouring, or patterns of colour, paying particular attention to markings which can be detected at long range.

Behaviour Visual clues, such as the way an animal moves on the ground, a bird's flight or perching behaviour, and audible signals such as call-notes or the sounds created by wing-beats are all important in species recognition.

Habitat and seasonal pattern As all species show some kind of preference for where they feed or seek shelter, the local habitat is a clue to the species which might be found there.

Knowledge of a species' habitat preferences taken together with any seasonal migration movements enables the sportsman to anticipate, within broad limits, which species he is likely to encounter at a particular locality. But general distribution limits such as 'normal' habitat and 'usual' range cannot be used alone as diagnostic features.

THE QUARRY SPECIES

The most popular quarry birds and animals which may be hunted by authorised persons are described in detail in this section.

Current legislation provides for open shooting seasons or shooting by authorised persons of more than 60 species of wild birds and terrestrial mammals in the UK. This includes both traditional sporting quarry species such as wildfowl and gamebirds and animals shot for pest control purposes such as crows and rats.

Those animals regarded primarily as pest species are outside the scope of this book, which is concerned with the sporting quarry which may be taken with a shotgun. Thus the great and lesser black-backed gulls, herring gulls and several species of small mammal are excluded. Of the mammals, only four species are considered to be traditional quarry for sporting shotgun shooting.

Quarry birds and animals fall into several categories

WILDFOWL

These comprise ducks and geese, large numbers of which are migratory, visiting the British Isles during autumn and winter, returning in spring to northern breeding grounds.

Ducks

These are the most widespread and numerous wildfowl. Sexes are normally easily distinguishable. The male is usually highly coloured, except in eclipse plumage, while the female has characteristically drab plumage throughout the year. The nine quarry species of ducks (ten in Northern Ireland) can be usefully divided in two main groups according to their mode of feeding.

Dabbling ducks

This group comprises mallard, teal, wigeon, pintail, shoveler and gadwall. As their group name suggests, dabblers obtain food mainly from shallow water, paddling to stir up mud or 'up-ending' to sieve out food material from just below the surface. They tend to be agile on land. Mallard, teal and gadwall regularly feed on agricultural land, especially cereal stubbles in autumn, while wigeon chiefly graze on grassland and saltmarsh.

Species in this group are typified by the ease with which they take to the wing. This is an important escape strategy as birds frequently feed in small wetlands and damp woodlands. Teal will rise almost vertically from the surface. All fly easily and show considerable agility on the wing.

Most dabblers are typically night-feeders. Their normal routine is to use a safe roost site during the day, frequently on open water such as small to medium-sized ponds, and flight to feeding areas at dusk, returning to their roost at dawn. This generalised pattern may be complicated by local weather and feeding conditions and will vary with different species. Those feeding on the foreshore, such as wigeon grazing on grass saltings are governed largely by tidal cycles. Bright moonlight under clear skies during a full moon resembles daylight and can result in a complex pattern of movements between roost site and intertidal feeding areas. This period of bright moonlit nights is also exploited by inland ducks which similarly flight between roost and feeding areas during the night.

Wigeon

Diving ducks

This group comprises tufted duck, pochard, goldeneye and, in Northern Ireland, scaup. These species typically use deeper, open waters for both feeding and roosting, and one site can fulfil both functions. They dive to moderate depths to forage on plant or animal material from the water or bottom muds.

Goldeneye

Ducks in this group are highly adapted to swimming, and as a result they move with less ease on land than dabbling ducks. They are also slower in taking to the wing and have to patter along the surface to gain lift. Often they will swim away or dive to avoid danger, only taking flight as a last resort. They do flight to and from roost sites if these differ from feeding waters, and they often show a peak of activity in evening and early morning, resting in the middle of the night.

Geese

This group includes the UK's largest quarry bird species. It is divided into two sub-groups. The 'grey' geese (*Anser* species) include the greylag, pink-footed and white-fronted goose; they are basically grey and greyish-brown with typically fairly uniform plumage tones. The young of all grey geese look rather similar, generally lacking adult plumage characteristics, but as they tend to retain strong family ties during their first winter, problems of identification are reduced.

The 'black' or 'dark' geese (*Branta* species) tend to have a contrasting black or dark brown with white or light grey colouring. The Canada goose is the only quarry species in this group. Sexes are generally similar and indistinguishable in the field.

Geese typically feed during the day and roost at night although, as with ducks, tidal cycles and moonlight will alter patterns of movement, especially of those species using tidal areas for feeding. Flocks (skeins) normally fly in V-formation or straggly lines. Their call notes are highly characteristic, and hence are very important in species recognition.

Other waterbirds

Two species of the rail family, moorhen and coot, are found in a wide range of marsh and open water habitats. They are typified by bulky bodies and they swim with a jerky action.

WADERS

Waders are a diverse group of birds. Golden plover and common snipe (plus curlew and jack snipe in Northern Ireland) occur in coastal marshes, inland wetlands and on moors. The woodcock is regarded as a 'forest wader' in view of its affinity with woodland habitats and close relationship to snipe. Sexes are generally indistinguishable in the field.

Common snipe

GAMEBIRDS

Gamebirds comprise two main groups, divided according to their habitat preferences. All gamebirds are characterised by their mode of flight. They are largely ground-dwelling birds, and tend to fly only when it is necessary. When flushed from cover they take off noisily. Once airborne their flight is strong, direct and characterised by short bursts of whirring wing-beats alternating with gliding on downward-curved wings.

Lowland gamebirds

These are pheasant, red-legged partridge and the grey partridge. The grey partridge is native to the UK, while the others are introduced species. All are closely associated with lowland agricultural and woodland habitats. However, in recent years red-legged partridges have been released in areas of moorland fringe.

Pheasant and red-legged partridges are intensively managed, as is the habitat they live in, to provide enough birds for sporting shooting purposes. This involves both habitat management, such as provision of cover, and species management which includes the rearing and release of young birds and providing supplementary food.

Red-legged partridge

Grey partridge populations are managed largely through the provision of suitable habitat but the species is rarely present in sufficient numbers to provide a sustainable shoot. It is recommended that where grey partridge numbers are low that shooting of them should cease until their numbers recover.

Upland gamebirds

This group comprises three indigenous grouse species, the red grouse, black grouse and ptarmigan. All three have different habitat requirements. Red grouse are characteristic of open heather moors, black grouse are found typically in moorland and forest-edge habitats and ptarmigan on higher, rocky mountain tops. Black grouse are subject to similar recommendations on sustainable shooting as grey partridge.

PESTS
Pigeons and doves

Three species (woodpigeon, collared dove and feral pigeon) can be shot (under the general licences) with the woodpigeon being the most sought-after species. It is widely regarded as a pest by farmers in view of the large numbers which may congregate to feed on recently sown or ripening crops.

Corvids

The shootable species (under the terms and conditions of the general licences for pest control) comprise crow (both carrion and hooded), rook, magpie, jackdaw and jay.

Hooded crow

The crow family includes species which have long been regarded as a threat to game-rearing operations and wild bird populations. They can also provide exceptional shooting. They have a varied diet, and readily adapt to exploit available food resources, hence the problems resulting from their predation on eggs and young birds. Sexes are similar and indistinguishable in the field. Most populations are resident, but in some areas they undertake short movements outside the breeding season to avoid harsh weather or involving the dispersal of young.

Hare and rabbit

These closely-related herbivores are characterised by their long hind legs and long ears. They are capable of high speed and rapid changes in direction while running. The brown and mountain hares are traditionally considered as game species. The rabbit is a major pest, but is also a sporting quarry.

Squirrels

Only the grey squirrel is a quarry species. It is characterised by its long tail and tree-living habits. It is considered a sporting quarry, although it is most frequently shot to prevent damage to nesting birds and forestry. More recently it is being controlled to help preserve the indigenous red squirrel population.

THE FOLLOWING GUIDE GIVES DETAILS OF THE PRINCIPAL QUARRY SPECIES

WIGEON

Anas penelope

size: 46cm (18in)

Female   *Male*

Field identification

Medium-sized, short-necked dabbling duck. Basic plumage colour of male is grey, with buff forehead and crown and remainder of head chestnut; chest pinkish-brown, white under-parts; characteristc white shoulder patch readily seen in flight. Female plumage duller; brown plumage tinged rufous, white underside, green speculum fringed with white wing-bars. Short bill and dark pointed tail useful diagnostic characteristics.

Voice: highly distinctive whistling *whee-oo* of male, typically heard from flocks in flight; females virtually silent.

Habitat and distribution

Small British breeding population restricted to upland lochs, pools and streams in open moorland, bogs, wooded country and saltmarsh. Chiefly maritime outside breeding season, mainly on mud-flats and saltings; sometimes frequents inland flood-meadows especially in eastern England and Northern Ireland.

British population mostly resident, moving to coast in autumn with some south-westerly movements to Ireland. Passage and winter migrants, chiefly from Iceland, Scandinavia and northern Russia, mainly present September to April. Occurs in large numbers in south-west and north-east Scotland and sparsely in eastern and south-eastern England. Widespread in Northern Ireland.

Behaviour and feeding

Highly gregarious outside breeding season. Very large feeding flocks occur; often roosts in large numbers on sea, sand-flats, etc. Usually roosts during day, feeding at night, but may reverse pattern depending on prevailing tidal and weather conditions. Grazes predominantly on grasses, usually while walking over exposed vegetation, but frequently feeds from water surface. Takes mainly leaves, stems, roots, etc of grasses and herbs, seeds and some animal material.

Nests on ground in heather, bracken or rank grasses near wetlands.

Similar species

Female resembles other female dabbling ducks, especially shoveler, pintail, gadwall and mallard.

Shooting season

J	F	M	A	M	J	J	A	S	O	N	D
31								-1-	INLAND		
	20								FORESHORE		

Northern Ireland open season is 1 September to 31 January.

TEAL

Anas crecca
size: 36cm (14in)

Male   *Female*

Field identification

Very small, compact dabbling duck. Male characterised by conspicuous grey plumage contrasting with dark chestnut head, creamy-buff patch on each side of black under-tail coverts and prominent white strip along scapulars; at close quarters broad green patch extending from in front of eye to nape bordered by narrow buff line is evident; the breast cream spotted with black; underside white. Speculum of both sexes green and black, bordered white. Female plumage mottled brown with paler cheeks and whitish underside. Juvenile similar to female, but more spotted under-parts.

Voice: Male has characteristic low, whistling *crick-crick*; female generally silent, but utters harsh *quack* in alarm.

Habitat and distribution

Breeding birds favour rushy moorland and heathland pools, bogs, etc, typically around small upland waters, but frequently well away from open water. In lowland areas prefers small lakes, rivers, fresh and brackish marshes with good cover. Requires shallow muddy water areas for feeding. In winter and on passage extends to coastal habitats (estuarine flats, salt marshes, etc) also larger freshwater areas.

Breeding population largely resident, moving south or south-west in autumn. Some migration from southern England to western Europe and Mediterranean. Large influx of passage migrants and winter migrants originate from Iceland, Baltic and North Sea countries, Scandinavia and northern Russia. Main winter concentrations are in south-east England; migrants appear from the end of August to November, returning March to early May.

Behaviour and feeding

Extremely agile in flight, frequently in tight packs; rises vertically from water or land and flies fast with characteristic very rapid wing-beats; long distance flights normally high, in lines or V-formation. Gregarious outside breeding season, often in small flocks; more dispersed in small parties, pairs or singly while feeding. Feeds primarily at night, often moving several miles from safe day-time roost to feeding area. Food obtained by dabbling in shallow, muddy water. Diet varies according to season and locality; seeds predominate in autumn and winter; increasing amount of animal material taken in summer.

Nests in thick cover on ground, normally close to water.

Similar species

Only species of similar size is garganey (protected) – a summer visitor.

Shooting season

J	F	M	A	M	J	J	A	S	O	N	D
31										INLAND	
	20							-1		FORESHORE	

Northern Ireland open season is 1 September to 31 January.

MALLARD

Anas platyrhynchos
size: 58cm (23in)

Male   *Female*

Field identification

Large dabbling duck. Adult male characterised by glossy, dark green head, white collar and purple-brown chest; rest of plumage mainly light grey, tail white with black central feathers. Female dull, mottled brown. Both sexes have purple speculum bordered by white wing bars, particularly conspicuous in flight. Juvenile similar to female.

Voice. Female has characteristic loud, deep *quark* either uttered singly (often in alarm) or several strung together during courtship. Male quieter; typical call a soft, nasal *quark* and high whistle.

Habitat and distribution

One of the most widespread of breeding birds, and the most numerous breeding waterfowl. Frequents a very wide variety predominantly still, shallow freshwater and brackish wetlands, from small ponds and large reservoirs to marshes, rivers, park lakes and canals. Outside breeding season extends to maritime habitats. Captive-bred birds released on a large scale to supplement wild stock. Breeding population mainly resident; local movements and dispersal of young predominate, although released stock recorded as migrants as far afield as Russia. Passage migrants and winter visitors include migrants from Iceland, Scandinavia, northern Russia and north-central Europe, but chiefly from Baltic and North Sea countries; normally present September/October to April/May, widespread throughout the country in both coastal and inland areas.

Behaviour and feeding

Typically feeds at night, resting by day at safe roost sites. Rises easily and almost vertically from water when flushed; flies quickly with shallow wing-beats. Flies in loose flocks, pairs or singly. Highly gregarious; males flock during breeding season, while female incubates; large flocks occur in autumn and winter.

Diet very varied, including wide range of plant and animal material; highly opportunistic feeder. Food obtained from water by sieving and pecking at surface, up-ending and occasionally diving. Usually nests in undergrowth close to water; readily accepts artificial nest structures.

Similar species

Colouring of male resembles male red-breasted merganser (protected). Female similar to females of other dabbling duck species, particularly gadwall, pintail, shoveler and wigeon, but both male and female are bigger and more heavily-built than other dabbling ducks.

Shooting season

J	F	M	A	M	J	J	A	S	O	N	D
31								-1-	INLAND		
	20								FORESHORE		

Northern Ireland open season is 1 September to 31 January.

PINTAIL

Anas acuta
size: 56cm (22in)

Female   *Male*

Field identification

Large slim-built dabbling duck with noticeably long neck and extended central pair of tail feathers forming characteristic needle-tail of male, and shorter but still pointed tail of female. Male has dark brown head, and back of neck, contrasting with pure white breast, sides and front of neck, extending as white streak up side of head: Under-parts white; back and flanks light grey; rump black; wings grey and brown with green speculum conspicuous in flight. Female duller, with grey-brown plumage and no discernible wing-pattern in flight, except a light trailing edge to inner wing. Juvenile resembles female, but generally darker and more uniform.
Voice: generally silent; male has low teal-like whistle, female has a hoarse *quack*.

Habitat and distribution

Small breeding population widely distributed in a diverse range of habitats, including moorland pools, freshwater marshes and damp, rough grassland in low-lying areas, preference for large estuaries. Very limited inland. In winter chiefly a coastal species, found mainly in estuarine and other sheltered coastal areas; also on inland flood-lands and freshwater marshes, and sometimes agricultural land.
Mainly migratory: breeding birds move south, but possibly remain within the UK; augmented in autumn by passage migrants and winter visitors from Iceland, Scandinavia and north-western Russia. Migrants appear in mid-September, departing in April with a peak in December in Britain and October to December in Northern Ireland.

Behaviour and feeding

Highly gregarious outside breeding season; flocks vary in size from small parties to several thousands on larger waters. Typically feeds at night and remains relatively inactive during daylight. Swims high on water; feeds mainly by up-ending or dabbling. Flight is fast and direct with rapid wing-beats; often fly in long lines or V-formation.
Diet includes a wide variety of plant and animal material chiefly from bottom mud in shallow water with a preference for small snails. Will also feed on stubble grain or dig plant roots and underground stems. Nests on ground usually in short cover; often in loose colonies; primarily on islands in lakes and adjacent to moorland pools.

Similar species

Although male readily distinguished, female resembles other female dabbling ducks, particularly mallard, gadwall, shoveler and wigeon.

Shooting season

J	F	M	A	M	J	J	A	S	O	N	D
31									INLAND		
	20							-1	FORESHORE		

Northern Ireland open season is 1 September to 31 January.

SHOVELER
Anas clypeata
size: 51cm (20in)

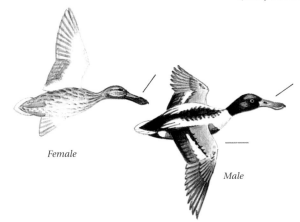

Female

Male

Field identification

Medium-sized dabbling duck; both sexes characterised by large spatulate bill, large head and short neck, which are readily discernible both in flight and on the water. Male has striking pattern of dark green head, chestnut flanks and belly contrasting with pure white chest, which is noticeable at considerable distances; pale blue fore wing, green speculum edged with white. Female primarily mottled brown, with similar but duller blue fore wing and green speculum. Juvenile a dull version of female.

Voice: generally silent outside breeding season.

Habitat and distribution

Breeding population thinly but widely distributed; main concentration in southern and eastern England. Restricted chiefly to shallow, nutrient-rich fresh and brackish waters throughout the year. Birds migrate south to France, Spain and into Africa; large numbers pass through the UK on migration; smaller numbers overwinter. Migrants and passage migrants originate from Iceland, Scandinavia and Russia. Local birds normally leave by late October; main passage through the UK occurs in November; main return movements March/April.

Behaviour and feeding

Characteristic appearance when swimming, with front end carried low and huge bill angled down. Feeds primarily by swimming with head and neck submerged and surface feeding, moving head from side-to-side filtering out food particles; occasionally up-ends. Most carnivorous dabbling duck but diet varied, including microscopic animals, seeds and other plant material. Predominantly a daytime feeder usually singly, in pairs or small flocks. Flight agile with rapid wing beats; makes loud whistling noise in flight; wings appear set well-back on body; rises easily from water with characteristic drumming sound. Particularly active on the wing in April. Nests usually close to water, on ground in variety of habitats from rushes to open, short grassland and low scrub.

Similar species

Huge bill distinctive, but plumage of female similar to that of female gadwall, pintail, mallard and wigeon.

Shooting season

J	F	M	A	M	J	J	A	S	O	N	D
31									INLAND		
	20							1	FORESHORE		

Northern Ireland open season is 1 September to 31 January.

GADWALL

Anas strepera
size: 51cm (20in)

Male   *Female*

Field identification

Medium-sized dabbling duck. Male has uniform grey-brown plumage and conspicuous black rump; distinctive white speculum forms a bold white patch on trailing edge of wing, readily seen in flight; wing coverts chestnut and black. Female dull, mottled brown, with white belly and white wing patch as male. Juvenile much like female, but well marked with streaks and spots on underside and darker upper-parts.

Voice: Female has high-pitched *quack*; male has a short nasal call.

Habitat and distribution

Prefers shallow, nutrient-rich, sheltered lakes, slow-moving streams, and lowland freshwater marshes; outside breeding season also found on brackish and saline waters. Establishment in the UK as a breeding species aided by escapes from collections and release of captive-bred birds. English population mainly resident, but Scottish birds move southwards to England and Ireland and some movement of birds from East Anglia to western Europe and Mediterranean. Winter visitors chiefly from Iceland, Baltic and North Sea countries; arrive mainly October/November, returning March/April. Northern Ireland population restricted to Lough Neagh and Strangford Lough. British population shows strong south-east preference.

Behaviour and feeding

Tends to be fairly secretive and retiring throughout the year; rarely gathers in large flocks; frequently mixes in small numbers with other dabbling ducks. Swims high in water; very mobile on both land and water, as well as in air. Flies with rapid beats of apparently pointed wings, producing whistling sound in flight. Normally a daytime feeder; may spend much time flying between roost and feeding sites. Feeds mainly on aquatic plant material, obtained either by swimming with head under water or dabbling; also steals food from other waterbirds; will occasionally feed on land, grazing and taking grain from stubble fields.

Nests on ground, close to water in very dense vegetation.

Similar species

Size close to that of mallard; female plumage resembles female mallard, pintail, wigeon and shoveler.

Shooting season

J	F	M	A	M	J	J	A	S	O	N	D
31									INLAND		
	20							1	FORESHORE		

Northern Ireland open season is 1 September to 31 January.

TUFTED DUCK
Aythya fuligula
size: 43cm (17in)

Female

Male

Field identification

Small diving duck. Adult male black with white flanks and belly; long, thin, drooping crest. Female rich dark brown head and back; flanks and underside paler; crest shorter than in adult male. In flight both sexes appear black with white belly and a distinctive broad white wing bar. Juvenile resembles female.
Voice: virtually silent except during courtship.

Habitat and distribution

Commonest UK diving duck. Frequents open fresh waters of all sizes. During breeding season prefers more secluded, small to moderate-sized lakes, particularly with fringing reeds or similar cover and vegetated islands. In winter readily takes to larger open waters such as reservoirs. Rarely found on sea. Widespread breeding species throughout lowland areas. Marked range extension and population increase in recent decades; readily colonises new breeding habitats created by gravel excavation, etc. In winter local populations show some southerly movement within the country. British population augmented by birds from Iceland, northern and western Europe. Migrants usually arrive mid-September/mid-November, depart late February/mid-May, and are found throughout the UK, with notable concentrations on reservoirs in south and east England.

Behaviour and feeding

Frequently uses same water area for both feeding and roosting, thus avoiding need to flight to and from feeding sites. Feeds mainly morning and evening. Normally shifts position if disturbed before flighting off water. Patters for some distance on take-off; flight usually straight and rapid, with quick beats of short wings. Dives in generally shallow waters; food mainly animal material (molluscs), supplemented by vegetation (grasses, duckweed, etc).
Nests typically close to water in bushes or rushes; occasionally found in loose colonies, especially on islands.

Similar species

Male resembles male scaup (protected except in Northern Ireland); female similar to female pochard and scaup.

Shooting season

J	F	M	A	M	J	J	A	S	O	N	D
31									INLAND		
	20							1	FORESHORE		

Northern Ireland open season is 1 September to 31 January.

POCHARD
Aythya ferina
size: 46cm (18in)

Male

Female

Field identification

Medium-sized diving duck with 'dumpy' appearance on water. Male has dark chestnut head and neck contrasting with pale grey back and flanks, black breast and tail. Female uniform dull brown, slightly paler around face. Both sexes characterised in flight by absence of white on wings; pale grey wing bar runs full length of wing, forewing dark grey. Juvenile resembles female.
Voice: virtually silent except during courtship.

Habitat and distribution

Common wintering species, but sparse breeding population. Favours larger lowland lakes, sluggish streams, etc, with dense fringing vegetation, and preferably islands. Found on larger freshwater areas, such as reservoirs, in winter, rarely in brackish or maritime habitats. Most birds resident, but move away from breeding areas in winter; some migrate to western Europe and Mediterranean. Passage migrants and winter visitors occur mainly during October to April; widely distributed, but with large concentrations in central lowlands of Scotland, central and southern England.

Behaviour and feeding

Gregarious outside breeding season, normally in small parties, occasionally flocks of several thousands. Spends most of time on water; take-off from water laboured, but when airborne has strong, fast flight with rapid beats of short wings making whistling sound. Flocks normally fly in tight group; long distance flights in lines or V-formation. Rarely occurs on land. Roosts during day in flocks on open water; feeds day and night but less actively in middle of night. Diet mainly vegetable matter, including seeds, stems, leaves, etc, obtained normally by diving, occasionally by up-ending in shallower water. Nests on ground elevated above surface on rush or reed base.

Similar species

Male readily distinguished; female resembles female tufted duck and scaup (protected except in Northern Ireland).

Shooting season

J	F	M	A	M	J	J	A	S	O	N	D
31									INLAND		
	20							1	FORESHORE		

Northern Ireland open season is 1 September to 31 January.

GOLDENEYE
Bucephala clangula
size: 46cm (18in)

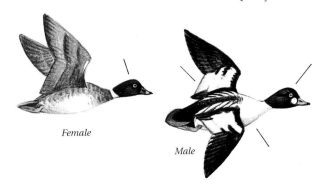

Female

Male

Field identification

Medium-sized diving duck. Male has high-crowned, dark head with greenish-purple gloss and circular white patch on cheek; neck and under-parts white contrasting with black back and rump and grey tail; extensive white on inner wing readily seen in flight. Female smaller than male; has chocolate-brown head, pale blue-grey upper-parts with white under-parts, grey flanks and tail; wings dark with conspicuous white patch similar to male. Juvenile closely resembles female.
Voice: generally silent, except during courtship display.

Habitat and distribution

Breeding habitat is tall forests close to moderately deep, productive open waters. During passage and on migration will make use of a variety of open water – lakes, reservoirs, streams, estuaries, etc. Migratory, but small breeding population in northern Scotland possibly undertakes only local movements; migrants mainly from Scandinavia, arrive from mid-September and return March/early May. Mostly coastal distribution over winter, but widespread inland. Often associated with pochard. Very common on Lough Neagh and Lough Beg in Northern Ireland.

Behaviour and feeding

Gregarious outside breeding season, normally in small flocks; spends most time on water or in flight, rarely comes to land. Mainly diurnal feeder; roosts frequently considerable distance from feeding area. Flies with rapid wing-beats creating a characteristic loud whistling. Feeds chiefly on animal material, especially molluscs, crustaceans and insect larvae, obtained by diving to middle depths or bottom of feeding water. Commonly associated with outflows from sewers, breweries and processing plants.
Nests in holes in trees; readily takes to nest boxes.

Similar species

Both sexes readily distinguished from other diving-duck species.

Shooting season

	J	F	M	A	M	J	J	A	S	O	N	D
31										1-	INLAND	
	20										FORESHORE	

Northern Ireland open season is 1 September to 31 January.

GREYLAG GOOSE

Anser anser

size: 75-90cm (30-35in)

Sexes similar

Field identification

The largest grey goose. Head, neck and most of body uniform pale brownish-grey. Characterised by large size, heavy head and neck with stout bill, and very pale blueish-grey forewing – the latter especially obvious in flight. Bill bright orange with no black, and a white nail, legs flesh pink. Breast often spotted with black. Young birds similar to adults, but generally unspotted, with greyer legs.

Voice: like domestic goose; a deep, loud nasal call; flight call loud, characteristically a deep *cackle*.

Habitat and distribution

In summer grazes in a variety of wetland habitats from lakes and marshes, agricultural pasture, to upland bogs and moorland. British breeding birds mostly resident. In autumn and winter migrants generally found on agricultural pasture and cultivated land, marshes and estuaries. Some local movements of breeding populations occur; main influx of Icelandic-breeding birds to Scotland occurs in late October, and departure is generally mid-April. Highest concentration of migrants is found in east-central Scotland and the northern Scottish isles. Local in Northern Ireland.

Behaviour and feeding

Flight rapid and powerful with regular beats of broad wings; characteristic circular flutter of wings on landing; takes off with ease from ground, although with more difficulty from water. Usually flights from roosts to feeding grounds in early morning. Gregarious outside breeding season. Largest flocks usually occur in autumn when feeding on stubble and potato fields. Often found in mixed flocks with pink-footed geese where winter ranges overlap. Feeds almost entirely on plant material, normally grazing on land, but will feed on water, up-ending for submerged material. In autumn and winter normally feeds on grassland, cereal root crops, etc; late spring diet includes growing cereals.

Nests on ground either amongst heather (Scottish moors and bogs) or in bushes, reedbeds or other dense vegetation providing shelter; especially on islands; often colonial and rarely far from water.

Similar species

Can be confused with bean (protected), pink-footed and white-fronted geese (especially immature birds), but all are smaller and more slightly built by comparison; calls are also distinctive.

Shooting season

J	F	M	A	M	J	J	A	S	O	N	D
31									INLAND		
	20							-1-	FORESHORE		

Northern Ireland open season is 1 September to 31 January.

PINK-FOOTED GOOSE

Anser brachyrhynchus
size: 60-76cm (24-30in)

Sexes similar

Field identification

Medium-sized, grey goose characterised by dark head and neck, contrasting with pale brownish body. Bill is small and short, dark coloured with a pink band; feet and legs are pink. Back and wings grey; paler forewing noticeable in flight. Young birds darker and more uniform above, mottled appearance below compared with more uniform colouring of adults.

Voice: characteristic short, high pitched flight notes; also lower, more musical nasal calls.

Habitat and distribution

Breeding range in Arctic, from east Greenland and Iceland to Svalbard. Birds visiting the UK originate mainly from Iceland, nesting in coastal areas of south-central Iceland and north-east Greenland. Winters in northern Britain and Ireland, with main concentrations in eastern Scotland and northern England. Limited numbers in Northern Ireland. Arrives in September/October and departs April/May. Found mainly on arable land, roosting on sand and mudflats in estuaries, inland lochs or reservoirs in moorland adjoining feeding areas.

Behaviour and feeding

Autumn and winter flocks may comprise several thousand birds. Tend to feed by day but occasionally (especially under full moon) will stay out well into night or flight out to feed by night and roost during the day. Roost sites may be several miles from feeding area. During autumn feed mainly on barley stubble, potatoes and sugar beet. Pastures used throughout winter and in spring feeds exclusively on grass and winter cereals; carrots and brassicas are taken in some districts.

Similar species

Can be confused with greylag, bean (protected) and white-fronted geese (especially immature birds); voices are characteristic.

Shooting season

J	F	M	A	M	J	J	A	S	O	N	D
31								-1-	INLAND		
	20								FORESHORE		

Northern Ireland open season is 1 September to 31 January.

WHITE-FRONTED GOOSE

Anser albifrons
size: 66-76cm (26-30in)

Sexes similar

Field identification

Two races of the white-fronted goose regularly occur in the British Isles, the European white-front (*Anser a. albifrons*) and Greenland white-front (*A. a. flavirostris*). The two sub-species are distinguishable in the field and have markedly different winter ranges. The following description relates to the European white-front, as current legislation does not provide for an open season for white-fronts in Scotland or Northern Ireland, where the majority of the Greenland sub-species occur. The Greenland race wintering in Wales is subject to a voluntary moratorium by BASC wildfowling clubs because of declining numbers.

Medium-sized grey goose characterised by white band at base of upper bill and black barring on belly. Amount of black on underside extremely variable. Young birds lack these characteristics, but are normally found in the company of adults. Generally dark greyish-brown plumage, fairly long, pink bill and orange legs.
Voice: generally noisy species; typically high-pitched, musical *cackle*; flight call normally two or three syllable, short metallic notes.

Habitat and distribution

Breeding range in northern Siberia, within the Arctic Circle. Western section of population winters in Baltic and North Sea countries. Winter haunts located in south and east-central Wales and in southern England (Greenland white-front occurs in Scotland, Ireland and in west-central Wales). Arrives during October to January; departs March/April. Found mainly in lowland wet grasslands and marshes, arable fields, etc.

Behaviour and feeding

Normally feeds during day, usually close to roost and in undisturbed conditions will roost on feeding area. Congregate on arable land in autumn, feeding primarily on grass and stubble grain. Other food recorded includes potatoes, weed seeds and clover. Flight noticeably more effortless than other grey geese; quicker and more agile on the wing and can take off almost vertically when disturbed. Large flocks gather on migration, but tend to split more readily into family parties and smaller groups than other grey geese.

Similar species

Can be confused with greylag, bean (protected) and pink-footed geese (especially immature birds), but generally distinguished by small size, uniformly dark plumage, and distinctive 'musical' call notes.

Shooting season

J	F	M	A	M	J	J	A	S	O	N	D
31									INLAND		
	20								FORESHORE		

Protected in Northern Ireland and Scotland.

CANADA GOOSE
Branta canadensis
size: 91-102cm (36-40in)

Sexes similar

Field identification

Very large grey-brown goose; black head and neck with distinctive white patch extending from the chin across cheeks to behind the eye. Body dark above; paler brown flanks and under-parts; tail-coverts white, tail black. Bill and legs black. Young birds similar to adult, and generally indistinguishable in field.
Voice: considerable variety of calls, but flight note is characteristically a deep, loud, resonant, trumpeting *honk*.

Habitat and distribution

Introduced to England from North America in 17th century. Feral population generally resident, but local movements occur outside breeding season, and moult-migration to Scotland has evolved in Yorkshire sub-population since 1950s. Northern Ireland populaion mainly restricted to Strangford Lough and Lough Erne. Found in variety of lowland wetland habitats from ornamental park lakes (where first established) to freshwater marshes, gravel pits, etc; frequently close to human habitation.

Behaviour and feeding

Feeds mostly during day; grass is prime constituent of diet throughout the year, supplemented by some insect matter in summer. Will also take clover and cereals; and sometimes up-end in water to feed on submerged vegetation. Gregarious, especially outside breeding season. Flight fast, with deep, regular wing-beats; often flies at low levels. Frequently walks from roost site to feeding area.
Usually nests on ground; prefers islands in open waters or marshes.
Nest is normally under bushes or other sheltered spot. Frequently colonial, but pairs highly territorial and aggressive.

Similar species

Not easily confused with other species of geese. The largest European goose: much larger than brent and barnacle (both protected), with characteristic black and white pattern on head and neck.

Shooting season

J	F	M	A	M	J	J	A	S	O	N	D
31									INLAND		
	20							-1	FORESHORE		

Northern Ireland open season is 1 September to 31 January.
Canada geese are also included on certain general licences in England throughout the year.

MOORHEN
Gallinula chloropus
size: 33cm (13in)

Sexes similar

Field identification

Small-sized, dark waterbird. Striking white flank stripes and under-tail coverts contrast with dark brownish to black upper-parts and slate-gey under-parts. Bill and frontal shield bright red; yellow bill tip. Sexes similar; juveniles brownish with creamy flank stripes, white under-tail coverts and greenish-brown bill.
Voice: loud call notes include a sharp metallic *krick*.

Habitat and distribution

Breeding habitats include a wide variety of freshwater environments throughout most of the country; particularly in smaller ponds, ditches, sluggish streams, etc, but also in reed-beds, damp meadows and larger lakes often in towns and cities. Frequently feeds away from water in adjacent grassland, etc. Found on larger waters outside breeding season. Most British birds resident, but local movements occur; some migrants from western Europe occur mainly in eastern England during autumn and winter. Absent from upland areas of Britain and Northern Ireland. Commonest in southern parts of England.

Behaviour and feeding

Solitary, in pairs or small parties; may gather into larger flocks during winter. Swims with jerky head action and tail cocked; flicks tail when anxious. Quite reluctant to fly, often seeking cover when disturbed; takes off from water by pattering along surface; flies low and fast with rapid wing beats and trailing legs. May roost in trees and bushes. Feeds in water, pulling plant material, etc from surface, or walking through damp grassland. Diet varied; includes leaves, grass, seeds and fruit, also insects, eggs, earthworms, slugs, small fish, etc.
Nest usually in aquatic vegetation cover at waterside or close to water in adjacent undergrowth; normally constructed of dead reeds, sedge, etc.

Similar species

Only likely to be confused with coot.

Shooting season

J	F	M	A	M	J	J	A	S	O	N	D
31							1				

Protected in Northern Ireland.

COOT
Fulica atra
size: 38cm (15in)

Sexes similar

Field identification

Medium-sized bulky waterbird, characterised by overall very dark slate-grey body colour and black head in sharp contrast to white bill and frontal shield. On water distinguished by rounded back and apparently small head. Sexes similar, juvenile dark brown above, pale brown and whitish under-parts.
Voice: call a loud, sharp *kowk*.

Habitat and distribution

Inhabits mainly lowland open waters and slow-flowing streams. Normally requires minimum of a half hectare (one and a quarter acres) of open water for breeding territory. Prefers shallow, nutrient-rich waters. Very large flocks occur in winter on reservoirs and other large expanses of open water, especially in southern England. Breeding population largely resident, with some movement away from higher altitudes and northern areas outside breeding season. European birds overwinter in large numbers, mainly in eastern and southern England.

Behaviour and feeding

Highly territorial and aggressive in breeding season; gregarious at other times, winter flocks often congregating into large rafts. Swims and dives easily; normally reluctant to fly, but when forced to do so takes off from water by pattering along the surface in the manner of diving ducks. Flight normally low and ungainly with neck and legs extended; generally only flies for short distances. Obtains food mainly by diving to collect plant material from middle or lower depths; dives prolonged and food brought to surface to be consumed. In winter will also graze on damp grassland areas close to open water. Diet mainly leaves, stems, etc. of aquatic plants, also some animal material.
Nest normally found among aquatic vegetation fringing open water; constructed of dead leaves from tall marsh plants.

Similar species

Only likely to be confused with moorhen; frequently associates with diving ducks, but readily distinguished from these.

Shooting season

J	F	M	A	M	J	J	A	S	O	N	D
31							1				

Protected in Northern Ireland.

GOLDEN PLOVER

Pluvialis apricaria
size: 28cm (11in)

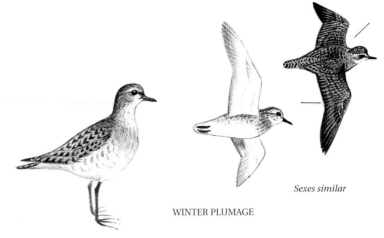

Sexes similar

WINTER PLUMAGE

Field identification

Medium-sized wader with short, straight bill and rounded head. Distinguished at all seasons by rich gold and black-spotted plumage on back and wings, white underwing, and dark tail; no wing bar. Face and underside in summer black with yellowish-white fringing stripe from forehead and neck to flanks. In winter underside and face whitish, mottled gold-brown. Juveniles more uniform than adults, paler above and darker below.

Voice: call note and characteristic clear, liquid *tlui* uttered in alarm, and normally in flight.

Habitat and distribution

Breeding birds typically haunt flat or gently undulating moorlands, upland grass-heaths and peat bogs. Move from hills in winter to lowland farmland and coastal habitats, occurring on arable and pasture farmland, estuaries, etc. UK population largely resident, moving to lowlands and coasts; supplemented by passage migrants and winter visitors mainly from Iceland and Scandinavia, during September to April or May. British breeding population in central and northern England, Wales and throughout Scotland. Northern Ireland population mostly over-winters in north-east Northern Ireland but breeds in the north-west.

Behaviour and feeding

Gregarious outside breeding season; normally found in flocks, frequently in association with lapwing (protected) on inland roosts and feeding sites. Flock flies in compact group; flight rapid and very agile. On ground has upright stance when still; walks with rapid steps tilting to gather food items.

Similar species

Confusion most likely with grey plover (protected), which is a winter visitor to coastal areas of the UK.

Shooting season

J	F	M	A	M	J	J	A	S	O	N	D
31							1				

Northern Ireland as Great Britain.

SNIPE
COMMON
Gallinago gallinago
size: 27cm (10¹/₂in)

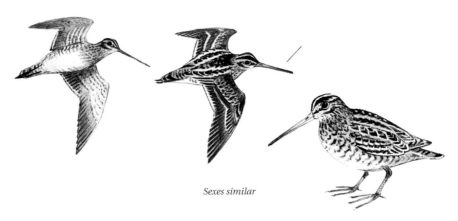

Sexes similar

Field identification

Small, brown wader with characteristic long, straight bill. Upper-parts rufous brown and black with golden-buff stripes on head and back; under-parts buff with dark brown markings and pale barred flanks.
Juvenile resembles adult.
Voice: when flushed normally utters a sharp, grating call note.

Habitat and distribution

Breeding habitat is typically wet grassland, bogs, marshes, etc, occasionally drier moorland sites. In winter frequents a wide variety of wetlands, including freshwater and salt-marshes, usually in lowland areas. Breeding birds largely resident, undergoing local movements mainly to lower ground, with some migration to western Europe. Passing migrants and winter visitors occur, frequently in large numbers, during September to April, originating chiefly from Iceland, Scandinavia, Baltic states and western Russia.

Behaviour and feeding

Generally secretive. Normally rests during day in rank vegetation, feeding most actively at dusk. In winter feeds more freely in open and during daylight. Small flocks may gather outside breeding season in feeding area. Crouches when disturbed, often rising only when closely approached; characteristic, zig-zag flight when flushed, frequently drops down to cover rapidly from considerable height. Food chiefly animal matter, including worms, molluscs and insects.
Nests on ground in tussocks of grass or rushes, occasionally amongst heather.

Similar species

Most easily confused with jack snipe (protected but not in N. Ireland), which is much smaller and characteristically rises silently, very reluctantly (normally at walker's feet) and pitches down into cover after short flight. Woodcock somewhat similar to snipe, but larger with stouter bill and heavier build.

Shooting season

J	F	M	A	M	J	J	A	S	O	N	D
31							12				

Northern Ireland open season is 1 September to 31 January.

WOODCOCK
Scolopax rusticola
size: 34cm (13¹/₂in)

Sexes similar

Field identification

Medium-sized, dark round-winged wader with long straight bill. Plumage richly marked with browns, buff and black on upper-parts; under-parts light brown with fine dark brown barring. Exceptionally well-camouflaged while at rest in woodland; in flight looks stout with short tail and long bill angled downwards. Sexes similar; young resemble adults.
Voice: virtually silent except during roding flights in spring and early summer.

Habitat and distribution

Essentially a woodland wader; breeding habitat typically dry, deciduous woodland with open, damp grassland areas for feeding; also in mixed broad-leaved and coniferous woodland and forestry plantations in northern parts of range. In winter retains affinity for woodland cover and open areas to feed. Breeding population largely sedentary, with some local movements. Autumn migrants from Scandinavia, Baltic states and western Russia normally arrive in the UK in mid-October to mid-November, overwintering mainly in western and southern districts; return migration mainly March to mid-April.

Behaviour and feeding

Solitary and secretive. Rests during day in woodland ground vegetation. Flushed birds fly rapidly, dodging and weaving, and dropping quickly to cover again; rise with distinctive 'swish' of wings. Crepuscular, making regular flights to feeding grounds at dusk; also feeds in daylight in adverse weather conditions. Diet mainly animal material; earthworms of particular importance, also insects and larvae; uses long bill to probe deeply into soft ground to extract food.
Nests within woodland, often by trunk of tree or fallen branch, frequently in more open areas amongst bracken or brambles.

Similar species

Distinguished from snipe by larger size, heavy appearance, thick bill, and to some extent by habitat preferences.

Shooting season

J	F	M	A	M	J	J	A	S	O	N	D

-31-
1 ENGLAND & WALES
1 SCOTLAND

Northern Ireland season as for England and Wales.

PHEASANT

Phasianus colchicus
size: Male 76-89cm (30-35in)
      Female 53-64cm (21-25in)

Female

Melanistic

Male

Field identification

Large gamebird; both sexes characterised by long, pointed tail. Male colouring very variable, but typically iridescent copper body plumage with glossy dark green head, scarlet wattle and white neck ring. Female about 30 per cent smaller than male, duller, mottled plumage tones varying from light buff to dark brown. Juvenile similar to adult female.
Voice: male has a characteristic harsh, resonant crowing call; female less vocal, but utters soft whistle when flushed.

Habitat and distribution

Mainly a lowland bird favouring wooded agricultural land, parkland, etc; wild population also frequents more open habitats, particularly marshes and occasionally moorland. Resident; extensively released into areas managed specifically for shooting.

Behaviour and feeding

Very conspicuous, feeding in open, often in wet pastures and cultivated land adjacent to woodland. Tends to avoid flying unless forced; noisy take-off and strong flight with whirring wing beats, flight usually direct and rapid but seldom sustained; will fly hard and fast for short period, then glide towards cover. Gregarious, often gather in flocks to feed; sexes frequently segregated. Normally roosts in trees; also takes to trees to avoid danger. Feeds on wide variety of plant and animal matter including seeds, fruits, green shoots, leaves, insects, earthworms, slugs, etc.
Ground-nesting usually in dense cover of tall grass, hedgerow, scrub, etc.

Similar species

Large size and long tail are unmistakable characteristics; a wide range of colour variants occur; confusion can occur with feral birds of introduced species, particularly golden and Lady Amherst's pheasants.

Shooting season

| J | F | M | A | M | J | J | A | S | O | N | D |

Northern Ireland open season is 1 October to 31 January.

GREY PARTRIDGE
Perdix perdix
size: Male 31cm (12in)
       Female 29cm (11½in)

Female

Male

Field identification

Small, rotund gamebird with short wings and short, rufous tail. Sexes essentially similar, although male slightly larger; both have characteristic orange-chestnut face, grey neck and under-parts and chestnut flanks; male has conspicuous dark chestnut horseshoe patch on lower breast, but this feature usually only poorly developed in female. Juvenile has orange or chestnut markings replaced by brown streaking.
Voice: usual call a loud, high-pitched, grating *kirr-ic*.

Habitat and distribution

Found principally in mixed farmland areas preferring extensive tracts of grassland with fringing hedgerows, rough grass and some open ground. Mainly restricted to lowlands, but does occur up to 600m (2,000ft) on moors and grass heaths adjacent to cultivated land. Frequently occurs in sand dunes, marshes and bogs.
Resident, with some local dispersal in autumn and winter months. Very limited in Northern Ireland. Absent from western Scotland and most of western Wales.

Behaviour and feeding

Almost exclusively ground-dwelling; normally walks or runs with rounded back and head low, but runs for cover with neck stretched up. Often crouches when alarmed; flies reluctantly, but when flushed flight is strong and rapid with groups keeping well together.
Gregarious outside breeding season, with flock structure retained from early August to late winter. Pairs strongly territorial in breeding season. Feeds largely on plant material; females feeding young also take insects. Main components of diet are grass, leaves, cereals and clover, grain and other plant seeds.
Nests on ground in hedgerows, scrub or rough grassland; also in arable crops and cultivated grassland.

Similar species

Easily confused with slightly larger red-legged partridge; in particular juveniles of the two species are very similar and difficult to separate. Quail (protected) is similar, but much smaller.

Shooting season

J	F	M	A	M	J	J	A	S	O	N	D

Northern Ireland open season is 1 September to 31 January.

RED-LEGGED PARTRIDGE

Alectoris rufa
size: Male 34cm (13½in)
        Female 32cm (13in)

Sexes similar

Field identification

Small, rotund gamebird with short wings and tail. Sexes have similar plumage, but male slightly larger than female. Adult has distinctive long white eye-stripe, white throat and cheeks bordered black; chestnut, white and black barred flanks; red bill and legs; rest of plumage olive brown, grey and buff. Juvenile lacks distinctive head pattern and barred flanks.

Voice: call-note of male a low, harsh *chucka chucka*; both sexes utter sharp, barking *kuk-kuk* when flushed.

Habitat and distribution

Prefers dry, lowland areas, especially sandy heaths, chalk downs and open fields on light soils with low vegetation; occurs in a variety of habitats from open woodland to arable fields and pasture.

Introduced species; resident and largely sedentary.

Frequently released for shooting, and on an increasing scale in recent years. Most common in central, southern and eastern England.

Behaviour and feeding

Normally walks or runs quickly over open terrain; may roost in trees as well as on ground. Flies very reluctantly, and coveys inclined to scatter when flushed from cover; flight typical of gamebird species. Gregarious outside breeding season; frequently in large flocks (over 50 birds). Solitary and in pairs during breeding period. Feeds largely on plant material – particularly grain, weed seeds, leaves, also roots (eg. of sugar beet) and legumes; insects taken in late spring.

Nests on ground, usually sheltered by tussocks of vegetation, bush, rocks, etc.

Similar species

Easily confused with grey partridge, especially in flight. Quail (protected) is very much smaller, with duller plumage.

Shooting season

Northern Ireland open season is 1 September to 31 January.

RED GROUSE

Lagopus lagopus scoticus
size: Male 36-39cm (14-15½in)
Female 33-36cm (13-14in)

Sexes similar

Field identification

Medium-sized grouse characterised by rotund appearance, short wings; body plumage uniform dark rufous brown with darker wings and black rounded tail. Sexes closely similar, but female more barred and a duller rufous colour. Adults appear greyer in winter, with white under-wing coverts and occasionally show white on flanks and belly. Juvenile generally like female.
Voice: call when flushed a loud, crowing *kok*.

Habitat and distribution

Primarily associated with open upland moorland and bogs dominated by heather; also in grass heaths with heather or other dwarf shrubs. Highest densities occur on well-managed heather moor on rich soils, giving optimum supply of food and shelter, mainly in eastern parts of range; poorer soils and preponderance of wet grassy heaths in west result in lower numbers. Resident, moves to lower ground and occasionally cultivated land in winter. Very limited in Northern Ireland. Mainly restricted to central and northern England, and Scotland.

Behaviour and feeding

Basically a ground-dwelling bird, flies for short distances, usually close to ground unless driven higher. Flight strong and rapid, alternating between whirring wing-beats and gliding on decurved wings. Mainly gregarious outside breeding season; packs develop in early autumn as family parties disperse; normally up to 20 in a flock, occasionally more. Males become strongly territorial as winter progresses; non-territorial males and females remain in packs. Feeds almost exclusively on heather – particularly young shoots – throughout the year, but will take other plant material; insects may form a significant part of adult diet on blanket bogs and heather moors, and also taken by chicks at an early age.

Similar species

May be confused with female black grouse; ptarmigan always recognisable by smaller size and white wings and underparts.

Shooting season

J	F	M	A	M	J	J	A	S	O	N	D
							12				10

Northern Ireland open season is 12 August to 30 November.

BLACK GROUSE

Tetrao tetrix

size: Male 53cm (21in)

Female 41-43cm (16-17in)

Female

LEK DISPLAY POSTURE

Male

Field identification

Medium-sized grouse. Sexes dissimilar. Male (blackcock) plumage glossy blue-black with white wing bar and curled, 'lyre-shaped' outer tail feathers. Female (greyhen) warm brown above, greyer and paler underparts, mottled and barred with black throughout; forked tail. Male in eclipse plumage during autumn looks drab, without characteristic lyre-shaped tail. Juveniles like small dull female.

Voice: male usually silent away from lek; female call-note a loud *tchuk*.

Habitat and distribution

Prefers margins of hilly moors, adjacent to woodlands (including conifer plantations), marshes, bogs, etc. Typical habitat includes scattered groups of trees with good cover, and clearings for display grounds. Resident; male particularly sedentary; females and juveniles seldom move great distances. Absent from Northern Ireland and southern England.

Behaviour and feeding

Flight strong and rapid, usually over short distances only; frequently higher than other moorland gamebirds, but low in cover; often circles both on take-off and landing. Gregarious throughout the year, especially males; large winter flocks can occur. Perches in trees, feeds in trees in winter; roosts and feeds on ground in summer. Feeds chiefly on plant material throughout year; summer diet includes leaves and shoots of ground plants, seeds, berries, fruits, etc, and some insects. Autumn and winter food primarily shoots and buds of birch and Scots pine.

Nests on ground in close vegetation.

Similar species

Male unmistakable, but female may be confused with female red grouse or capercaillie. Confusing hybrids between black grouse and capercaillie, red grouse and pheasant occur.

Shooting season

Does not occur in Northern Ireland.

PTARMIGAN

Lagopus mutus
size: 33-36cm (13-14in)

Male & Female

WINTER PLUMAGE

Female
SUMMER PLUMAGE

Male
SUMMER PLUMAGE

Field identification

Small grouse; both male and female characterised by pure white wings and under-parts at all seasons. Three distinct seasonal plumage variations. In winter both sexes pure white except for black tail. Male in summer has dark greyish-brown and black mottled head, neck, flanks, upper breast and upper body and black tail; female browner with tawny markings. Male in autumn replaces dark plumage with paler colours, tail remains black; female darker. Juvenile like autumn female, but with pale brown wings and tail same colour as back.
Voice: call notes a low, grating *croak* and repeated *cackling*, often as alarm.

Habitat and distribution

Resident, restricted to arctic-alpine heaths in northern Scotland. In summer found on high-level, open rocky or stony terrain with abundant bilberry and cranberry; generally above 600m (2000ft) in Cairngorms, at lower elevations further north; moves to lower ground in winter.

Behaviour and feeding

Frequently tame and easily approached; flies reluctantly, preferring to crouch and skulk, relying on camouflage to avoid detection. Flight typical of grouse family, but fast and will fly up and down steep slopes quickly and easily. Food is almost entirely plant matter, mainly shoots, leaves and berries of heathland plants, also buds, twigs and seeds of trees like birch where available. Diet varies with seasonal availability of foods; will dig through snow in winter to get to food plants.
Nests invariably on ground; generally in open, partly sheltered by rock or taller vegetation.

Similar species

Characteristic white wings and underbody, together with habitat preferences, easily distinguish ptarmigan from other British grouse species.

Shooting season

J	F	M	A	M	J	J	A	S	O	N	D
							12				10

Does not occur in England, Wales or Northern Ireland.

WOODPIGEON

Columba palumbus

size: 41cm (16in)

Sexes similar

Field identification

Large, heavy pigeon characterised by broad white band across wing seen readily in flight, and white patches on sides of neck. Sexes similar. Body plumage basically blue-grey, head and neck bluer than rest, flanks and underside paler; purple-green gloss to sides of neck. Juvenile duller and lacks white on wings and neck. Voice: characteristic rhythmic, muffled cooing calls.

Habitat and distribution

Chiefly occurs in cultivated areas and woodlands, but also in towns and cities. Feeds on farmland and uses trees and hedges to roost and nest. Breeding population mainly resident, with local movements particularly influenced by farming patterns.

Behaviour and feeding

Normally feeds during daylight on ground in open cultivated land or woodland glades; makes extensive use of agricultural crops particularly in autumn and winter, including spilt grain on stubble, turnips, brassicas, clover, etc; also takes buds, young leaves and flowers in spring. Gregarious outside breeding season; commonly feeds in very large flocks; roosts communally in woodland or hedgerows. When flushed rises with loud clatter of wings; strong flight usually direct and rapid. Nest site varies, but normally in woodland or hedgerow trees; occasionally building, rock ledges, rarely on ground.

Similar species

Confusion most likely with stock dove, rock dove and some domestic pigeons (all protected), but all are smaller and lack white wing and neck patches of woodpigeon.

Shooting season

J	F	M	A	M	J	J	A	S	O	N	D

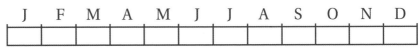

Can be controlled for specific purposes, under the terms of the general licences, by authorised persons throughout the year.

CROW

Corvus corone
size: 47cm (18½in)

Sexes similar

CARRION CROW   HOODED CROW

Field identification

Two races of this large corvid occur in the British Isles. The carrion crow (*C.c.corone*) has uniform sleek black plumage with a greenish or blue-purple gloss. The hooded crow (*C.c.cornix*) is black except for grey back and under-parts. Both have a heavy, dark brown bill, and square tail.
Voice: characteristic harsh, croaking *caw.*

Habitat and distribution

Carrion crow resident; population augmented by some winter migrants from western Europe. Breeding range overlaps with hooded crow in north and east Scotland, where hybrids frequently occur. Hooded crow resident in Scotland. Winter visitors from Baltic and Scandinavia occur mainly in eastern and central England during October/November to March/April. Found in a wide range of habitats from open moors and heaths, pasture and arable farmland, to parkland, wooded country, and coastlands. Hooded crow rare in England.

Behaviour and feeding

Relatively solitary, and most frequently found singly or in pairs; very occasionally in small flocks, particularly at roosts. Flight usually direct with slow deliberate wing-beats; rarely soars. Feeds chiefly on the ground in open country, walking or occasionally hopping while it forages. Crows are opportunist feeders and diet consequently differs with area and time of year; extremely varied food includes vegetable matter, carrion, small mammals, birds and eggs, amphibians, insects, etc.
Trees preferred for nesting, but will use low bushes, cliff ledges or on ground (usually on islets).

Similar species

Hooded crow unmistakable, although flight silhouette like carrion crow. Carrion crow may be confused with rook; other black corvids are the much larger raven (protected), and smaller chough (protected), both of which have very distinctive calls.

Shooting season

J	F	M	A	M	J	J	A	S	O	N	D

Can be controlled for specific purposes, under the terms of the general licences, by authorised persons throughout the year.

ROOK
Corvus frugilegus
size: 46cm (18in)

Sexes similar

Field identification

Large, black corvid with characteristic bare, white face patch. Loose plumage around flanks gives 'shaggy trousers' appearance. Feathers have iridescent blue-purple or greenish gloss; slender, pointed bill is grey-black. Juvenile birds lack bare face patch, but characterised by loose flank feathers.
Voice: wide range of calls, but typically a fairly soft *kaw*.

Habitat and distribution

Common throughout the UK except the Scottish Highlands. Chiefly found in agricultural areas with suitable nesting trees. Forages in both pasture and cultivated land. Commonly close to small settlements, mainly in lowlands largely absent from urban areas. Birds resident; population supplemented by influx of winter migrants from Scandinavia and central Europe, particularly to eastern Britain during October/November, departing late February/April.

Behaviour and feeding

Highly gregarious throughout the year. Normally encountered in small parties or flocks up to several hundred birds; in autumn and winter often roosts in very large numbers, frequently with jackdaws.
Flight direct with regular, rapid wing-beats; sometimes glides and soars; flocks fly in loose formation. Walks easily, hopping occasionally. Feeds in open on the ground. Diet chiefly comprises vegetable matter, especially cereals, root crops, fruits, etc; animal food mostly gathered from grassland, primarily earthworms and leatherjackets obtained by probing the top layer of soil. Will also take a variety of invertebrates, carrion, small mammals, young birds and eggs.
Nests colonially, at traditional sites; normally in large trees, but not within extensive woodland areas; exceptionally on man-made structures. Most frequently uses beech, oak, elm, Scots pine and sycamore trees.

Similar species

May be confused with carrion crow. Some resemblance to raven (protected) and chough (protected), but these have distinctive call notes.

Shooting season

J	F	M	A	M	J	J	A	S	O	N	D

Can be controlled for specific purposes, under the terms of the general licences, by authorised persons throughout the year.

JACKDAW
Corvus monedula
size: 33cm (13in)

Sexes similar

Field identification

Small, dark corvid, characterised by grey nape and ear-coverts; under-parts dark grey, remaining plumage black. Distinctive pale grey eye, and short bill.
Voice: characteristic short, high-pitched, metallic *tchak.*

Habitat and distribution

As rook, frequents a wide variety of relatively open habitats, from parkland and farmland to sea-cliffs, towers and old buildings, etc. Forages mainly in pasture land. Population generally sedentary, although some local movements and migration to Continent recorded. Winter migrants from Europe appear during October/November to late February/April.

Behaviour and feeding

Highly sociable corvid, often in large flocks and frequently associates with rooks and starlings when foraging in pastures. Moves on ground with quick, jerky walk; appears more alert and 'perky' than other corvids. Highly adaptable, omnivorous feeder; diet varies considerably with location and time of year. Spends much time feeding on surface insects in grassland; grain and wild plant seeds form an important part of vegetable matter eaten. Also takes legumes, earthworms, birds' eggs and nestlings, and carrion.
Usually nests in a hole in tree, building, rock face, etc; also constructs nest in trees.

Similar species

Most likely confusion is with chough (protected), but this species has distinctive flight and call-notes. Carrion and hooded crow, raven (protected) and rook all much larger and heavier than jackdaw.

Shooting season

J	F	M	A	M	J	J	A	S	O	N	D

Can be controlled for specific purposes, under the terms of the general licences, by authorised persons throughout the year.

MAGPIE

Pica pica
size: 46cm (18in)

Sexes similar

Field identification

Medium-sized corvid, characterised by distinctive black and white plumage and long wedge-shaped tail (comprising 50 per cent of total length). Belly, flanks and scapulars white; rest of plumage black with bluish or greenish gloss. Sexes alike; juvenile a duller version of adult.

Voice: an unmistakable harsh, loud, repetitive *chak-chak-chak*, easily heard at long range.

Habitat and distribution

Common and widespread but absent from Scottish Highlands and Islands. Resident; chiefly in farmland and open country with hedges and trees, also urban parks, suburban gardens, etc.

Behaviour and feeding

Found singly, in pairs or small parties; some flocking occurs; in autumn and winter roosts. Flight direct, with rapid wingbeats. Feeds primarily on ground, walking or hopping, and usually close to cover, in woodland rides, adjacent to hedgerows, etc. Diet varied, including insects, carrion and vegetable matter, especially grain, berries, fruits, etc; preys on nests containing eggs and young of small birds; takes small birds and mammals, and a variety of molluscs, earthworms, etc.

Prefers nesting in tall trees and bushes, commonly ash, oak, hawthorn, sycamore and alder; will use cliffs and crags if no suitable trees available; nest of sticks and earth frequently domed with thorny branches.

Similar species

Both adults and juveniles unmistakable, with distinctive plumage and voice.

Shooting season

J	F	M	A	M	J	J	A	S	O	N	D

Can be controlled for specific purposes, under the terms of the general licences, by authorised persons throughout the year.

JAY
Garrulus glandarius
size: 34cm (13½in)

Sexes similar

Field identification

Medium-sized corvid, characterised by white rump, black tail and white wing-patch conspicuous in flight. Body pinkish-brown; bright blue and black barred wing covers; black and white erectile crown feathers; fairly long tail and short, rounded wings.

Voice: characteristic harsh, screeching call, very loud and detectable over long distances.

Habitat and distribution

Scarce/absent from central and northern Scotland and west and north-west Northern Ireland. Primarily an inhabitant of oak woodlands, but found in a variety of fairly open deciduous woodlands and coverts with good secondary growth, also mixed and coniferous woods, suburban gardens and parks, orchards, etc. Birds mainly resident, but local movements do occur; winter migrants from Baltic and North Sea countries of continental Europe – often resulting from invasion movements rather than regular migratory movements – recorded mostly in south-east England.

Behaviour and feeding

Rarely outside woods; moves in tree-canopy by jumping among branches; usually hops on the ground. Flies easily among trees, but in open flight appears weak and laboured with jerky, flapping action. Commonly in small parties or flocks outside breeding season.

Acorns predominate in autumn diet, and large numbers stored for winter feeding, hence close association with oak woodlands; other vegetable matter includes fruits, also grain and legumes; animal food includes young birds and (especially) eggs, and woodland insects.

Nests in trees, in more secluded parts of broadleaved or coniferous woodland.

Similar species

Easily identified by voice and plumage characteristics plus habitat preference.

Shooting season

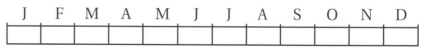

Can be controlled for specific purposes, under the terms of the general licences, by authorised persons throughout the year. Protected in Northern Ireland.

BROWN HARE

Lepus europaeus
size: 50-68cm (20-27in)

Field identification	Medium-sized mammal characterised by very long ears and long hind-legs. Ears have black tips; body colour yellowish to reddish brown in summer, becoming greyer in winter; upper tail is black.

Habitat and distribution

Primarily a lowland species: prefers open, relatively flat country, especially farmland, and also deciduous woodland. Extends to higher moors in some areas, where range overlaps with mountain hare. Introduced into Ireland but localised distribution. Scarce in Cornwall and north-west Scotland.

Behaviour and feeding

Mainly nocturnal and solitary. Moves very fast over the ground, leaping with legs fully stretched; frequently zig-zags, especially when bolting if disturbed from form. Feeds on a wide range of vegetation, including agricultural crops – and young forestry plantings.
Form may be in tall grass, scrub, woodland or open fields, and is normally well-sheltered.

Similar species

Resembles mountain hare and similar to, but much larger than, the rabbit.

Shooting season

J	F	M	A	M	J	J	A	S	O	N	D

Northern Ireland open season is 12 August to 31 January.
In Great Britain restrictions apply on moorland and unenclosed land, see page 44.

MOUNTAIN (BLUE) HARE

Lepus timidus
size: 45-55cm (18-22in)

Field identification

Two sub-species occur - Scottish blue hare and Irish hare. Medium-sized mammal characterised by long, black-tipped ears, and long hind-legs; tail lacks any black colouring. Body colour grey-brown to reddish-brown in summer; in winter largely white with black ear-tips, although not all individuals change colour, and in Ireland none attain white coat; during moult mixtures of white and grey-brown (or blueish-brown) occur.

Habitat and distribution

Mainly found in upland areas, but also on lower ground in Ireland (where it largely replaces the brown hare). Absent in Wales. Inhabits both open hillsides and mountain habitats, and woodlands, including forestry plantations.

Behaviour and feeding

Normally fairly solitary, but may be found in small groups. Often active during daylight. Moves with leaping gait; when running tends to take a fairly direct line with little zig-zagging. Feeds on a wide variety of vegetation, including the bark and tops of young trees, occasionally inflicting serious damage on plantations. Form normally amongst boulders or rocks, or grass tussocks.

Similar species

Mountain hare (except in winter coat) closely resembles brown hare, and is similar to the much smaller rabbit.

Shooting season

J	F	M	A	M	J	J	A	S	O	N	D

Protected in Northern Ireland.
In Great Britain restrictions apply on moorland and unenclosed land, see page 44.

RABBIT

Oryctolagus cuniculus
size: 34-45cm (13-18in)

Field identification

Medium-sized mammal characterised by long ears and long hindlegs; short, woolly tail which is white on underside contrasting with black or brown-grey above. Body colour normally light brown, but wide range of colour varieties occur, notably black, fawn, white and silver-grey.

Habitat and distribution

Very widely distributed on farmland, heaths, sand dunes, moorland, etc; also in woodland; generally not at higher elevations. Local variations in population densities are greatly influenced by outbreaks of myxomatosis and viral haemorrhagic disease.

Behaviour and feeding

Most active in evening, also feeds during afternoon and at night. Moves with bounding gait; runs quickly, turning at sharp angles. Burrows extensively (only the doe actually excavates); lives colonially in warrens; occasionally lives above ground (especially young bucks). Feeds mainly on grass and other green herbage; frequently causes damage to farm and garden crops when local population is high; will gnaw tree bark, especially in winter and with a preference for saplings.

Capable of breeding throughout year, but mainly spring and early summer; young born in burrow dug away from main colony.

Similar species

Both brown and mountain hares are larger, with longer ears and larger hindlegs.

Shooting season

J	F	M	A	M	J	J	A	S	O	N	D

In Great Britain restrictions apply on moorland and unenclosed land, see page 44.

GREY SQUIRREL

Sciurus carolinensis
size: 45-55cm (18-22in)

Field identification

Medium-sized rodent. Characterised by long, bushy tail (nearly half total length); grey fur with some reddish and yellow tinges on back and flanks; and absence of prominent ear tufts. Under-parts white; gains silver-grey winter coat usually in late autumn, and shorter, brownish summer coat in spring.

Habitat and distribution

Very widely distributed. Introduced into the UK during late 19th and early 20th centuries; widespread by 1950s. Chiefly in deciduous woodland, particularly with oak, beech, chestnut and hazel. Also parkland, suburban gardens, etc; mainly in lowland areas; less frequently in coniferous woodland.

Behaviour and feeding

Active during the day, particularly in early morning. Moves quickly on the ground with bounding gait. Varied diet includes grain, herbage and animal material. Plant components of diet dominated by nuts and other tree seed (including beech-mast), also leaves, buds, shoots, etc; strips bark to eat woody tissue (inflicting damage in the process); animal material includes small birds, nestlings and eggs; also takes insects and fungi.

Similar species

Resembles red squirrel (protected), although the latter is smaller, richly coloured, more lightly built and mainly found in coniferous woodland.

Shooting season

J	F	M	A	M	J	J	A	S	O	N	D

6 – *ROUGH SHOOTING*

The term 'rough shooting' embraces all forms of sporting shotgun shooting other than formal driven game shooting and coastal wildfowling. It therefore includes the pursuit of game, pigeons, rabbits, hares, snipe and inland duck and geese, though some forms of shooting, such as pigeon decoying, are considered by many to be distinct from traditional rough shooting.

This type of shooting can provide some of the most demanding and exciting sport to be found in the UK. As with any form of shooting, to be successful you must understand the habits of your quarry and these are explained briefly in the chapter on quarry identification.

Good rough shooting can be enjoyed on a relatively small area of land, dependent upon the type and distribution of habitat. The way you shoot will largely be determined by the nature of the ground and the available quarry. As ever, permission from the landowner or occupier is needed before entering land to shoot.

GAME

Rough shooting for game is normally undertaken by a small group of shooters, walking in line, with dogs working the ditches, hedgerows or a field of root crops. It is particularly important to ensure that a shoot leader or captain is appointed, so that every member keeps their place in the line, and that the line is kept straight, which is particularly important for safety.

WILDFOWL INLAND

Most rough shoots either provide, or have the potential to provide, an opportunity for inland duck shooting. If suitable ponds or wetlands do not exist they can be created.

The best opportunities for inland duck shooting come from either flighting a pond at dusk or by intercepting birds as they flight between their roosting and feeding areas. Good duck shooting can also be enjoyed when duck, particularly mallard, flight onto stubble fields during September and early October. This can be done at night, particularly for a few nights either side of the full moon, when there may be sufficient moonlight and a light cloud covering against which the birds will be clearly silhouetted.

If part of the land floods after prolonged rainfall, keep an eye open for preened feathers and droppings. If these signs of duck occur, then be prepared to take advantage of the fortuitous opportunity for flighting in that area. The rough shooter's opportunity to pursue geese inland will be largely restricted to those which roost on reservoirs and lakes; to lie in wait for them under their flight lines can be most exciting.

Snipe can provide some of the most testing shooting for the rough shooter and may be walked up or, most difficult of all, flighted at dusk as they come to a marshy spot to feed.

RABBIT SHOOTING

The rabbit population has recovered in many parts of the country following the decline caused by myxomatosis in the 1950s, but is still affected by it and more recent diseases.

There are various ways of shooting rabbits but the most common, with a shotgun, is to flush them out of hedgerows or cover with a dog. Local knowledge can be important in identifying the place where rabbits are most likely to be found, from which side of the hedgerows they are more likely to bolt and from which cover they are likely to be flushed. If rabbits are not walked up with a dog they can be stalked, or ambushed as they emerge from their burrows to feed at evening time.

They can also be flushed from their burrows with ferrets, but no rabbit should ever be shot at the mouth of a burrow. It should always be allowed to get a short distance from the burrow before being shot as a wounded one may well crawl back down the hole. It may then be unrecoverable, will suffer and be wasted.

WOODPIGEON SHOOTING

Woodpigeon, feral pigeons and collared doves shot under the terms and conditions of the general licences can give exceptional sport and provide a cheap and tasty meal.

The main methods of shooting are decoying, roost shooting and flight lining. The method chosen will depend on the time of year, the agricultural crops in the area and the type of countryside over which you are shooting.

Decoying is the main method used by the majority of pigeon shooters. It can be enjoyed all the year round, depending on the types of agricultural crops in the area. A good knowledge of the pigeon's behaviour and its diet are very important, however it is reconnaissance to find out where they are feeding and resting that makes a successful pigeon shooting outing.

Roost shooting is primarily a winter activity and involves getting underneath the flight line of birds approaching the woodland or copse where they are going to roost for the night or rest during the day.

Pigeon shooter in hide

A CODE OF CONDUCT FOR ROUGH SHOOTING

WHERE

Always ensure that you are authorised to shoot where you intend to go and that you know precisely where the shoot boundaries are located

You should be aware of any public rights of way crossing the land over which you are shooting and ensure that no users are frightened or endangered.

Always advise the owner and/or tenant in good time if you want to go shooting and check that it is convenient

WHAT

Always confirm with the owner and tenant what quarry you may shoot

An invitation to shoot over a piece of land will not necessarily entail an invitation to shoot all quarry species. It is important that you know precisely what species you may pursue.

Carry your shotgun certificate, or a photocopy of it, with you

EQUIPMENT

Ensure there is at least one competent dog present to retrieve shot game

Make every effort to retrieve shot game before moving on. Dead game left behind will be wasted, and if quarry is wounded you have an overwhelming duty to find the animal and humanely dispatch it as quickly as possible

Always have a dog to retrieve shot game

Always use suitably-loaded cartridges for your quarry

The combination of gun, cartridge, and choke is important, and will be influenced by personal preference (see page 27).

IN THE FIELD

Always ensure your companions know your position and all observe safe shooting angles

If shooting in company, appoint a leader and always ensure that each member of the group knows the plan for the day.

Always be especially vigilant about keeping in a straight line when walking in thick cover or dead ground

The going may be easy for you, but slow and difficult for your companions.

Always identify your quarry positively and ensure that it is safe to shoot before raising your gun

Make sure that you know what is beyond the target. Never shoot through or over obstructions as you do not know what is on the other side. If in doubt, do not shoot.

Shooting at quarry that is beyond your personal capabilities, whether game or pest species, can lead to unnecessary wounding and wastage: it is never acceptable.

Always condemn unsporting behaviour – that is shooting at birds which are out of range or those which are too close

Only shoot at birds and animals which are close enough to be killed cleanly – do not shoot at a high or distant target just in the hope of a 'lucky shot'

Always seek to approach your quarry as a sporting shot, giving it reasonable 'law'. This also means that a flushing dog (or ferret) is not endangered

'Law', in this context, means allowing the quarry to gain sufficient distance from you to present both a safe shot and provide unspoiled meat for the table.

Do not shoot where you (and your companions) may not be able to retrieve shot game, such as in dense cover, by flowing water or over property boundaries. Shot animals may suffer and will be wasted.

If a bird or animal is shot and falls beyond your boundary, it is essential to seek permission to retrieve it, even if you are using a dog

If it is sometimes impossible to prevent shot birds falling beyond a boundary, it is good practice to seek prior permission from neighbouring landowners to retrieve such birds or animals.

Never carry your gun onto someone else's land unless you have been authorised – that would be criminal trespass.

When shooting pests which are not necessarily destined for the human food chain, shooting at low or close birds is acceptable if done safely.

Avoid disturbing livestock

Never shoot at a bird just because it is in the range of your gun. It may provide a better opportunity for one of your companions

Never shoot at partially-obscured quarry. It can be difficult to identify or shoot cleanly the quarry if it is obscured and it may not be a safe shot

Always respect the owner's property, crops, livestock and fences and follow the countryside code

Open gates rather than climb them, and close them after you. Climb a secured gate at the hinged end. Never damage rails, fences or hedges. Never walk in standing crops/corn. Avoid disturbance to livestock. Keep your dog under control. Do not leave litter.

Never be greedy. Do not shoot more than you really need or you can put to good use

Where crop protection is concerned it may be necessary to take large bags of pest species, but you should always try to put them to good use.

Do not overshoot resident or migratory quarry birds; a viable population must be left at the end of the season

Particularly for wild pheasant shoots the unwritten rule is always to shoot more cocks than hens and no hens to be shot after Christmas.

AT THE END OF THE DAY
Never leave litter, take your empty cartridge cases home

If you have been shooting from a hide, make sure that the area is left in such a way that no one can tell that you have been there.

Always ensure that you have collected up all your equipment and leave the place tidy

It is courteous to thank the owner or occupier and to offer him something from the bag

Always take your quarry from the game bag as soon as possible. Store it in a cool fly-proof place. Do not waste it

Always attend to your dog before yourself

If the journey home is a long one, your dog may appreciate a drink before you leave.

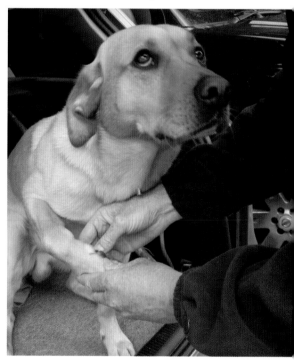

Always inspect your dog for thorns and cuts

Treat any injuries to your dog promptly.

Always clean your gun before putting it away. Check it over for faults which may need attention

Have all faults attended to immediately.

7 – *DRIVEN GAME SHOOTING*

Historically, game was shot by 'walking up' and shooting birds as they flew away, but in the mid-to-late 1800s, coinciding with the general introduction of breech-loading shotguns, a change occurred and the Guns stood while the birds were driven over them by beaters. Driven shooting became a formal branch of the sport around which a strict code of conduct, or etiquette, evolved.

The social and political upheavals of two world wars saw dramatic changes in the ownership of land, and game shooting is no longer the preserve of elite estates. Some shoots will be grand affairs, managed for the landowner's enjoyment or by letting days to visiting guns. But far more typical is the syndicate shoot where members rent the sporting rights over land and manage the shooting themselves. Regardless of the scale of operation adherence to correct etiquette is important.

Gamebirds, as defined by the Game Act 1831, are pheasants, partridges, red grouse, ptarmigan and black grouse. Ptarmigan are normally only shot when walking up, and are therefore outside the scope of this chapter.

WHERE AND HOW

Shooting rights over any piece of land are always legally held by someone. There is no set procedure for the management of shooting rights. It is up to the owner or the lessee of the shooting rights to decide which system suits them best.

Most formal shoots vary from about 400 up to several thousand acres in size.

There are many ways of managing game shooting rights. The most common are:
1. The landowner may retain the game shooting rights and organise the shooting for the benefit of himself and his guests.
2. The landowner may retain the shooting rights, but invite a number of outside Guns to pay to have a gun in the shoot for one season. This system helps the shoot owner defray the costs of running the shoot.
3. The landowner may retain the shooting rights and each season sell a number of shooting days to outside Guns who pay for one day's shooting. This again helps to defray costs.

4. The landowner may lease the game-shooting rights to an individual who then takes on the financing and running of the shooting in any way he wishes.
5. The landowner may lease the shooting rights to a 'syndicate' of Guns who take on the responsibility of financing and organising the shooting in any way they wish.
6. An individual, a group of people or a company (e.g. a sporting agency) may buy the shooting rights over one or more parcels of land in perpetuity or for a set period of time, and run the shooting in any way they wish.
7. A sporting agency may lease the shooting rights and sell shooting days to outside Guns.

WHEN

The open and close seasons for game shooting are defined by the Game Act (England and Wales) 1831, Game Preservation Act (Northern Ireland)1928 and Game (Scotland) Act 1772. Some so-called game species are covered by the Wildlife and Countryside Act 1981 or the Wildlife (Northern Ireland) Order 1985.

The open seasons are:

Shooting Seasons	England Wales & Scotland	Northern Ireland
Pheasant	October 1 – February 1	October 1 – January 31
Partridge	September 1 – February 1	September 1 – January 31
Red grouse	August 12 – December 10	August 12 – November 30
Black grouse (not currently found in NI)	August 20 – December 10	----
Ptarmigan (only found in Scotland)	August 12 – December 10	----
Common snipe	August 12 – January 31	September 1 – January 31
Jack snipe	Protected at all times	September 1 – January 31
Woodcock	October 1 – January 31	October 1 – January 31
Woodcock (Scotland)	September 1 – January 31	----

THE CODE OF GOOD SHOOTING PRACTICE

The Code of Good Shooting Practice 2008

This code, which is supported by BASC and all the main shooting and countryside organisations, sets out the framework that enables shoot managers, Guns, gamekeepers and their employees to provide sustainable shooting, paying attention to the management of habitat and avoiding nuisance to others. All who shoot, or are involved in shooting in any way, should abide by this code and remind others of its provisions. In particular you should remember The Five Golden Rules.

The Five Golden Rules

- Shooting must meet the standards described in The Code of Good Shooting Practice, show respect for the countryside and consideration for others.
- Shoot managers must endeavour to enhance wildlife conservation and the countryside.
- Respect for quarry is paramount. It is fundamental to mark and retrieve all shot birds. Shot game is food and must be treated as such.
- If birds are released, shoots should take steps to comply with the Game and Wildlife Conservation Trust's guidelines for sustainable releasing.
- Birds must never be released to replenish or replace any birds already released and shot in that season.

Copies of the Code are available from BASC 01244 573000 or from http://www.basc.org.uk/en/codes-of-practice/code-of-good-shooting-practice.cfm

SHOOTING ETIQUETTE

Always reply promptly to an invitation to shoot

Never bring a guest without first confirming that you may

Always remember that it is the sportsman's responsibility to understand the laws relating to his sport. In particular be able to recognise your quarry, know when and where you may shoot, and where lead shot is prohibited

Always arrive punctually

Always wear a hat, sensible footwear and suitable clothing to suit your surroundings

If you have not been told at the Guns' briefing, then ask your host what game is to be shot, and the position regarding ground game and pests

If you have not been told at the Guns' briefing, then ask how many Guns are shooting and, if you draw for a number, how the system works

At most shoots, pegs will be numbered 1-8; Number 1 is usually on the right and Number 8 on the left of the drive. The normal practice is to move up two numbers for each consecutive drive. Make sure you know what number peg you should go to for each drive.

Never be afraid to seek advice on any aspect relating to the conduct of the day

Always carry your shotgun certificate, or a photocopy of it, with you

Always keep your gun in its cover until you are about to shoot

A responsible shot will have third party liability insurance cover. BASC membership provides this.

A covered gun is especially important when moving to and from drives and while travelling in vehicles.

Always go to your stand quickly and quietly and check where the other Guns are placed

Acknowledge the Gun on either side of you, or any 'stops' or pickers-up, by raising your hat or hand, but not by calling out

Always check the direction the beaters will come from, the position of stops and where the pickers-up are placed

Always check if there is any agricultural work in progress in your vicinity or any public right of way

Always remain quiet at your peg, and do not move from where you were placed, unless so instructed by your host

Never load your gun until the drive commences and unload as soon as it is finished

Never take long shots, shoot where you cannot see that it is safe, or shoot at partially-obscured game

Never shoot low in front when the beaters are approaching

Never let excitement cloud your judgment

If you hit a bird make sure it is dead and recoverable before looking for another bird to shoot

Always 'mark' carefully all game shot to your gun, and collect birds near your peg at the end of the drive. If it is safe and permitted, collect fallen birds around you during a drive

Never turn to shoot behind without first taking the gun from your shoulder and raising the barrels to point vertically while you turn round, and then checking it is safe to fire

Never be greedy. Just because a bird is in range of your gun does not necessarily make it yours; it may produce a more sporting shot for one of your companions

Never shoot between drives

If shooting with a pair of guns, make sure you and your loader have practised the method of changing guns. The person passing the gun will hold it in his right hand at the grip with the barrels pointing upwards. The person receiving the gun will take it in his left hand by the fore-end. The safety catch should be on 'safe' throughout.

Either use your own dog, or tell a picker-up the numbers and whereabouts of lost or wounded game so that it can be quickly brought to hand and dispatched. A sharp knock on the head with a suitably heavy stick or priest is recommended.

GUNS AND CARTRIDGES
Always use cartridges which are suitably loaded for your quarry

Never leave litter at your peg

AT THE END OF THE DAY
Always thank the keepers, beaters and pickers-up as it is largely their efforts which have provided your sport

Always take care of any game which you have been given. Do not waste it

Always ensure that you have collected up all your equipment

Always thank your host for your day's sport, and, as an extra courtesy, write and thank him later

Always feed and water your dog before yourself and check over for thorns and cuts

Clean your gun, and check it for faults which may need rectifying. Have any faults attended to immediately by a competent gunsmith

Traditionally, different pellet sizes in lead shot have been favoured for game shooting such as:

    Grouse – 6/7
    Partridge – 6/7
    Pheasant – 5/6/7
    Woodcock – 7

Recent research, however, may result in such shot sizes changing, generally towards larger pellets than were used in the past. While the traditional game load has long been 30g or 32g (1¹/₁₆ oz and 1¹/₈ oz) of no.6 shot nowadays game shooters are using more no.5 or larger shot.

If lead shot cannot be used, a substitute like bismuth will be needed. This material has somewhat different ballistic characteristics as it is less dense than lead. In order to achieve pattern density and striking energy levels sufficient to ensure consistently clean kills, it is necessary to use at least one size larger (no.5 or larger in place of lead no.6).

Remember that relatively little choke is needed for game shooting.

The above relates to standard 12-bore loads, smaller bore guns may have shorter effective ranges.

It is customary to tip the headkeeper, but if in doubt check with your host.

8   –   *WILDFOWLING*

For many centuries duck, goose and wader shooting has been part of life on estuaries around our coast. The participant was and still is referred to as a wildfowler and he continues to follow old traditions established by professional wildfowlers.

Wildfowling is now purely a recreation, with sportsmen in pursuit of a limited number of quarry species. Normally the wildfowler goes on foot, but in some circumstances boats are used. Though it is a thoroughly modern recreation, it rewards the correct use of historic skills as well as the understanding of the natural world. The participant requires toughness and perseverance, but can be rewarded with highly-prized food for the table and an experience which is priceless.

Purists will argue that true wildfowling is strictly a coastal activity, taking place below the high-water mark, that is to say on the foreshore around the coast. However, duck and goose flighting does take place inland on marshes, lakes and specifically managed flight ponds throughout the country.

The foreshore in England, Wales and Northern Ireland

In England, Wales and Northern Ireland the traditional place for wildfowling is that part of the seashore which is more often than not covered by the flux and reflux of the four ordinary tides occurring midway between spring and neap tides. This is called the foreshore and much of it is in Crown ownership or subject to control by the holders of regulating leases from the Crown Estate. The remaining areas are generally in private hands.

Following an agreement between the Crown Estate and BASC, the Crown has encouraged wildfowling clubs to take leases of sporting rights on Crown Estate foreshore and BASC has actively assisted its clubs in this process. This has allowed for increased management of the foreshore and greater security for shooting. Any shotgun certificate holder seeking foreshore wildfowling can obtain information on local wildfowling clubs from BASC.

In addition BASC members can take advantage of the BASC's Wildfowling Permit Scheme which provides access to wildfowling opportunities throughout the UK. Details of this can be found at www.basc.org.uk or by calling BASC's wildfowling and wetlands officer.

The foreshore in Scotland

In Scotland the foreshore is defined slightly differently as the area between high and low-water marks of ordinary spring tides. In Scotland, whether the foreshore is owned by the Crown or a private individual, local authority or institution, the Crown retains in trust for the public certain rights on the foreshore, including that of recreation (except on Orkney and the Shetlands). As a result, members of the public may engage in wildfowling, and this public right may only be taken away by statute, for example by the establishment of statutory nature reserves or country parks.

In some such reserves and parks wildfowling continues to take place, but it is regulated by permit systems. The onus is on the wildfowler to establish whether statutory controls, or any permit system, exist in the locality.

UNDERSTANDING THE HABITS OF YOUR QUARRY

Ducks

Generally ducks feed by night and rest by day, flighting between feeding and resting places at dawn and dusk. On the foreshore ducks will also feed in daylight and their habits will be affected by the tide. The stronger the tide, the rougher the water and the more marked will be the movement of birds.

Geese

Geese feed by day and generally rest at night, flighting between their feeding and resting places at dawn and dusk. On moonlit nights, however, some species, in particular pink-footed geese, will flight back to their feeding grounds from their roost. The roost may be a large expanse of inland water or on the open shore or sea. During the period of the full moon they may even remain on the feeding grounds throughout the night.

Waders

Coastal wading birds feed on the intertidal zone, and their movement is largely based around the tidal cycle. Unlike snipe and woodcock, golden plover is the only wader species on the quarry list that regularly flights inland and feeds on pasture.

Teal shot on the foreshore

Coastal shooting

Successful wildfowlers rarely shoot many ducks or geese without acquiring a detailed knowledge of local conditions. This includes information about the prevailing and expected weather, the tides and their combined effect on the flighting and feeding habits of the birds. Making such observations, for which binoculars are an essential piece of equipment, can be every bit as fascinating as the actual shooting. The key to successful wildfowling is reconnaissance. Time spent observing the movements of wildfowl will provide the wildfowler the best chance of getting a shot.

At the beginning of the season the wildfowler will expect to see wildfowl and waders which have bred in the UK. At dawn and dusk mallard, teal and Canada geese will establish flight lines to and from their inland feeding grounds. At this time, since many mallard will be feeding inland, the wildfowler will endeavour to place himself strategically where he can intercept their flight.

By October the migratory duck and geese will have started to arrive in large numbers. Most estuaries are visited by small parties of migratory mallard, wigeon, teal and pintail, and in many areas of the UK there are wintering geese.

Once winter weather arrives, the wildfowler is in his element, for his best sport is often enjoyed when conditions are at their worst. Strong winds in particular keep the wildfowl on the move in an effort to find shelter, and when the inland freshwater marshes freeze up, wildfowl are forced to move to more open coastal areas.

In prolonged and severe wintry weather, hungry birds may lose body condition. At such times the true sportsman has no need to be told when to use restraint, but the Wildlife and Countryside Act 1981 empowers the Secretary of State, or his equivalent in the devolved governments, to invoke a statutory ban on wildfowling until the conditions have improved and the birds are fully recovered.

THE PRINCIPLES OF WILDFOWLING

Always know where you can shoot by understanding the definition of foreshore in the area where you intend to shoot

You must understand the definition of foreshore as given on pages 107-8. Ensure you get to and from the foreshore by legal rights of way or permission of the landowner.

Always know which species you may shoot and be capable of identifying them

Those who shoot on the foreshore can only legally take the birds listed in Schedule 2 Part 1 of the Wildlife and Countryside Act 1981 or the Wildlife (Northern Ireland) Order 1985, unless otherwise authorised.

Other species of birds which may be killed or taken at any time by authorised persons are covered by general licences although not many of these are likely to be encountered on the foreshore. You should be aware that some bye-laws, for example on nature reserves, may further restrict the species which may be taken.

Always know when you can shoot the quarry you intend to pursue

There are variations between the seasons in Great Britain and Northern Ireland. You will find details of all the seasons on pages 46 and 49.

The shooting of wildfowl on Sunday is illegal in some areas

In the past wildfowling was controlled by local authorities and as a result in some former counties and county boroughs in England and Wales there is no Sunday shooting of wildfowl. They are: Anglesey, Brecknock, Caernarvon, Cardigan, Carmarthen, Cornwall, Denbigh, Devon, Doncaster, Glamorgan, Great Yarmouth, Isle of Ely, Leeds, Merioneth, Norfolk, Pembroke, Somerset, Yorkshire (North Riding), Yorkshire (West Riding).

The counties referred to are those which were in existence before local government re-organisation in the early 1970s. It is the sportsman's responsibility to check whether or not Sunday shooting is allowed in the area where he wishes to go wildfowling.

There is no shooting of wildfowl in Scotland and Northern Ireland on Sundays or Christmas Day.

Guns and cartridges

Always choose a gun that is suitable for the type of shooting you intend to pursue. A double-barrelled 12-bore is a suitable all-round shotgun. If your fieldcraft is good, you can be successful with the standard 70mm (2³/₄ in) cartridge, though many wildfowlers prefer a 76mm (3in) or longer-chambered gun which enables them to shoot larger loads especially of steel shot more effectively. Big bore guns, i.e. 10, 8 and 4–bores, although capable of handling big loads effectively can be cumbersome and a burden.

The use of any gun or rifle firing a single bullet for the purpose of killing wildfowl, whilst not prohibited by law, is not an accepted sporting practice, and is discouraged by BASC. The use of semi-automatic shotguns for wildfowling is illegal unless they are incapable of holding more than two cartridges in the magazine.

In England and Wales it is illegal to shoot ducks, geese and waders with lead shot. It is also forbidden to use lead shot for any shooting on or over the foreshore and on or over certain listed sites of special scientific interest. In Scotland and Northern Ireland lead shot may not be used for shooting on or over wetlands.

Always choose a cartridge suitable for the type of shooting you intend to pursue

Steel, bismuth, tungsten-based and certain other shot materials are used in place of lead shot. Their characteristics are different from lead and different loads, shot sizes, components and shooting techniques may be needed. Extra care is needed with the hard shot types like steel or some tungsten-based types in different types of gun. The International Proof Commission (CIP) regulations guide their use.

A variety of non-lead shot is now available

Shot sizes

BB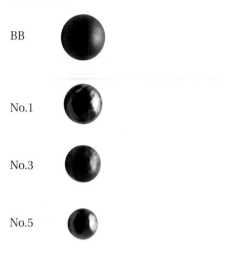

No.1

No.3

No.5

Comparative sizes of shot (treble actual size)

Traditionally, different pellet sizes in lead shot have been favoured for different types of shooting, such as:

Geese – BB/1/3
Mallard – 4/5/6
Teal/golden plover – 6/7

Recent research, however, indicates that shot sizes may need to change, generally towards larger pellets than were used in the past. This is to achieve a consistently higher level of lethality. Furthermore, each non-lead type has different ballistic characteristics. This means that pellet sizes may need to change further for these materials to achieve pattern density and striking energy levels sufficient to ensure consistently clean kills. In particular, where the material is less dense than lead, and so has less kinetic energy, it is necessary to use a larger size shot – for example, at least two sizes larger in steel (i.e. if lead no.6 then steel no.4 or larger), and at least one size larger in bismuth (no.3 or larger in place of lead no.4). For some of the more dense shot materials, such as some tungsten-based types, it may be possible to reduce pellet size and achieve higher pattern density as a result. This combination may well help to achieve high kill rates.

Remember that the cartridge must be compatible with the gun you are using, especially steel shot and the hard tungsten-based types. Always check the proof marks of your gun and if necessary seek the advice of a gunsmith.

Patterning

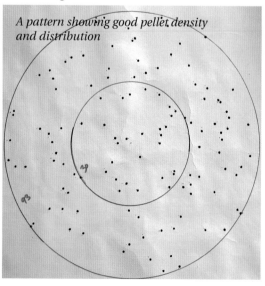

A pattern showing good pellet density and distribution

Each wildfowler should know how their gun 'patterns' with each chosen cartridge, i.e. whether the concentration of pellets on the pattern plate is dense enough to ensure, potentially, a clean kill of the target quarry. You cannot rely on books or published charts. The only way to be sure is to test cartridges of each type through your chosen gun/choke combination because every cartridge and every cartridge/choke combination is likely to pattern differently. Based on American research, an average pellet count in the standard 30inch circle of at least 65 pellets (of the appropriate size) is required for geese, at least 90 for large ducks such as mallard, 120 for medium-sized ducks such as wigeon, and 140 for small ducks such as teal.

Range

It is notoriously difficult to judge range accurately on the foreshore. Yet it is essential to know before shooting at what range you can shoot at, and expect to kill, your target quarry. This depends on your own skill and the capability of the gun/cartridge combination you use. Do not shoot further than either limitation or you are likely to wound rather than kill your quarry. If necessary practise range-judging beforehand and try to fix the distance of known features from where you are shooting so that you confine your shooting to that range.

PLANNING

Safety is paramount when planning a wildfowling trip: always plan your wildfowling outings very carefully

When you go on the foreshore for the first time, go in daylight with someone who knows the area and can point out marsh boundaries and any inherent dangers.

Always check the time of high and low tide before going on the marsh

Always avoid the more distant parts of the marsh when a big tide is expected. Remember that the time and height of the tide may be altered by weather conditions, particularly high winds. Tide tables give their times according to GMT so remember to make an hour's allowance if British Summer Time is still in force.

Always make sure you know of any local rules and restrictions

You should be particularly aware of those rules that may be operating in a controlled-shooting area such as a reserve where a permit scheme is in operation. It is the shooter's responsibility to find out about them before going onto a marsh.

Decoys not only attract quarry species but help to ensure that you shoot within range

EQUIPMENT
Always pay particular attention to your equipment: check its condition before going shooting

Essential wildfowling kit

Tide tables – always carry them with you in a waterproof bag.

Waterproof wristwatch – essential for judging the state of the tide.

Waterproof torch – but remember torch flashing is only justified in an emergency.

Binoculars – useful for identification purposes.

Wading pole – assists walking on the marsh, useful for sounding gutters and crossing places.

Pocket compass – to assist with working out direction, especially in mist or fog.

Mobile phone – in case of emergency.

Pull-through – a means of cleaning barrels if mud or snow enters them. A piece of rag on a cord is adequate.

If you are going out all day, carry some food and a thermos containing a hot drink.

Make sure you take necessary documents with you: shotgun certificate, or a photocopy of it; local permit (if applicable).

Wear comfortable, inconspicuous, warm, waterproof clothing. Waders are normally recommended.

A large canvas bag is not only useful for carrying shot wildfowl – particularly geese – but it is often handy to sit on.

A responsible shot will have public liability insurance cover.

Shooting from a boat

Remember it is illegal to shoot from a motorised boat. The engine must be switched off before shooting.

BEHAVIOUR ON THE MARSH
Always remember that the wildfowler's main quarry – wild geese and ducks – are largely migrants and as such are an internationally shared resource: we have a responsibility to help safeguard their populations and their environment

Remember that undue or continual human activity can cause unnecessary disturbance: you need not be shooting to cause a disturbance.

Always remember that others judge the sport of wildfowling by your behaviour

One foolish or irresponsible act brings the whole sport into disrepute. Do not disturb the locality, or other shooters, by making a noise or banging car doors when arriving early in the morning or leaving late at night.

Never arrive late or depart early in relation to flight times and do not disturb the shooting of those who have taken the trouble to get into position in good time.

Do not shoot in the immediate vicinity of houses adjoining the shore.

Make sure you are well hidden. Camouflage yourself to suit your surroundings.

Look through your gun barrels to make sure they are clear whenever an obstruction may have entered.

Take care to identify legal quarry: if in doubt, don't shoot.

Range judging when wildfowling is particularly difficult as the flight develops and light levels change; if in doubt that a bird is within your range, do not shoot.

Do not shoot where fallen birds cannot be recovered, such as over fast-running water or dense reed beds.

Shooting from a hide

Always be accompanied by a competent gundog

A dog is essential, especially for tide shooting and after dark, for retrieving shot birds, but must be kept under control at all times.

Try and make your dog comfortable. If you sit on your game bag, make sure that your dog also has a dry seat.

Always mark each shot bird, especially wounded quarry, and ensure that it is picked up and humanely dispatched

Send your dog to retrieve birds as they are shot. Do not look to shoot another bird before the first one has been retrieved, and, if necessary, humanely dispatched, as soon as possible. A sharp knock on the head with a suitably heavy stick or priest is most effective.

Searching the tideline with a dog after shooting will often recover lost birds (yours or somebody else's).

Never leave cartridge cases or litter on the marsh.

Never try to be clever waiting for the last moment to leave the marsh when the incoming tide is approaching. Channels fill quickly and in a very short time they can become a torrent.

ON LEAVING THE MARSH
Always consider the needs of your dog before your own

He may be cold and wet: dry him and provide him with a dog blanket or bedding to lie on, and food if necessary.

Always take care of your quarry

Ensure that shot birds are transported carefully and then stored in a cool, dry place. Do not waste them. If you are not going to eat your quarry give it to someone else.

Always pay special attention to cleaning your gun

Mud, salt water and drops of blood will quickly corrode it. Check it for faults which may need rectifying and ensure that is done before your next outing.

You can find a more detailed introduction to the sport in the BASC Handbook of Wildfowling published by Quiller.

9 – *THE ROLE OF GUNDOGS*

Whatever form of sporting shooting you engage in, your enjoyment will be increased by the presence of a well-trained gundog. There are very sound reasons why BASC strongly recommends that everyone who goes shooting should be accompanied by a competent gundog:

- By covering ground and searching undergrowth which is inaccessible to the shooter a gundog greatly increases the chances of finding and flushing quarry.

- A dog can quickly retrieve shot quarry so that dead game is not lost, and wounded quarry is despatched rapidly and humanely. No creature should suffer unnecessarily as a result of sporting or pest control activities.

- A dog is a wonderful companion and will make a shooting day more varied, interesting and enjoyable.

Gundog breeds

All breeds of gundogs have their supporters and good and bad examples of all breeds can be seen in the shooting field, so your choice is essentially a matter of personal preference. The following is an outline of the various breeds and how they are generally used, or the task for which they were bred.

Retrievers

The primary function of retrievers is to find and retrieve dead or wounded quarry, though they are often used for rough shooting and beating. Retrievers are used both by game shooters who stand at pegs and by pickers-up on driven game shoots. The four main types of retriever are:

Curly-coated retriever

Flat-coated retriever

Golden retriever

Labrador retriever

Of the four, the labrador is most often seen in the shooting field, and due to the nature of its coat, it is a good dog for the wildfowler as it is well protected against the cold.

Spaniels

Spaniels are used primarily to hunt ground and cover in order to flush quarry, but most will retrieve, so they are often used for picking up and are a favourite breed for rough shooting. By far the most popular is the cocker spaniel which comes in a wide variety of colours. The breeds in this group most often seen in the shooting field are:

English springer spaniel

Welsh springer spaniel

Cocker spaniel

Field spaniel

Clumber spaniel

Brittany spaniel

Irish water spaniel

Pointers and setters

The purpose of pointers and setters is to range in front of the Gun or Guns and to indicate the presence of quarry by adopting a rigid pose. This is called pointing. The breeds in this group most often seen in the shooting field are:

English pointer

English setter

Gordon setter

Irish setter

Hunt-point-retrieve breeds

These are multi-purpose gundogs, often referred to as 'HPRs', whose job it is to hunt, point, flush and retrieve. There are many breeds in this group and most have their origins in continental Europe. The most frequently encountered in the sporting field are:

German short-haired pointer

German wire-haired pointer

Vizsla

Weimaraner

Large Munsterlander

Spinone

Having considered the various breeds which are used for different purposes in the shooting field, it is up to the individual to decide which breed is most suitable for his type of shooting and circumstances.

Acquiring a gundog

If you consider your gun to be the most important piece of equipment, then certainly your dog comes a close second. You must therefore give great care and consideration to the acquisition of a gundog.

You may decide to buy a puppy, usually between eight and twelve weeks old, or to buy a part or fully-trained adult dog. The choice is up to you and will be governed by a range of considerations. It is not our intention here to explain how to set about training a gundog, but simply to make you aware of a number of basic points which you should consider before acquiring one. You must obviously think about kennelling, feeding, cost and the dog's need for exercise. All gundogs need to be kept fit and they require a considerable amount of regular exercise.

Basic training of gundogs

If you decide to acquire a puppy, you will also have to decide whether to train it yourself or whether you will send it away to be trained. If you decide to train the dog yourself, work out a programme or follow the recommendations offered by an experienced gundog trainer.

Briefly, basic training should consist of sitting to command, walking to heel, stopping immediately on command, stopping and sitting to shot (when the gun is fired), coming back when called, understanding the command 'No', observing directional hand signals, being steady to moving quarry and dropping to the flush of quarry.

Make sure that training sessions are enjoyable for both you and your dog. Formal training will not begin until a puppy is several months old but good manners can be taught from the beginning. Gundog training and obedience classes at local clubs can help you and your dog. BASC also runs a nationwide programme of training days. Mixing with other dogs will help steady and socialise a young dog.

Dog handling in the field

When out shooting with your dog, you should follow these guidelines:

Some basic points of law

- In Scotland and Northern Ireland you must have a game licence if you use your dog for picking-up game (the game licence in England and Wales was abolished in August 2007)

- All dogs (including gundogs) must, in public places, wear a collar marked with the owner's name and address except where the dog is being used for sporting purposes at the time

- Dogs must be kept on a lead when on a designated road except where the dog is being used for sporting purposes at the time

- It is an offence to have any dog dangerously out of control in a public place

- Gundogs must not be sent to retrieve game that has fallen beyond a shoot boundary without the prior consent of the adjoining landowner. To do so constitutes civil trespass

- Owners and handlers of dogs commit an offence if their dogs worry livestock on agricultural land

- Owners and handlers of dogs similarly commit an offence if their dogs are not under close control in a sheep enclosure (even if not worrying the sheep) except where the dog is being used for sporting purposes at the time

- If a dog kills or injures livestock, the keeper (owner or person in possession) is liable for damages to the livestock owner.

Dogs at home

- Provide your dog with living quarters that are warm, dry and draught-free

- Ensure that your dog has clean drinking water available at all times

- Feed good quality food appropriate to the dog's age and work regime

- Ensure that a new puppy is vaccinated to protect it against distemper, hepatitis, parvo virus, leptospirosis and tetanus

- Ensure that your dog receives an annual booster for parvo virus and leptospirosis and every other year for distemper, hepatitis, and tetanus

- Ensure that your dog is wormed regularly to control roundworms and tapeworms. This is particularly important if young children are around

- Ensure that an infestation of lice, fleas, ticks or ear mites is treated promptly. Remember to treat bedding, carpets and furniture used by the dog at the same time

Dogs in the car

- Never leave your dog unattended in a car unless absolutely unavoidable. If you have to do so, leave the dog for the minimum time, park in the shade and ensure adequate ventilation and provide drinking water

- Never leave a dog unattended in a car on a hot or sunny day. Even with the windows open a car can quickly become an oven

- Always carry water and a bowl in the car when transporting your dog

- Dogs should be confined within the vehicle so that they cannot interfere with the driver. BASC recommends that the dog should travel in a cage, dog box or custom trailer.

Dogs in the field

- Ensure that your dog will be welcome before taking him on a shoot or anywhere else that you visit

- Be confident your dog is under your control before you take him out in the field. An untrained dog is a nuisance and a possible danger to livestock, other dogs and people

- Never take a bitch in season (oestrus) to a shoot where there will be other dogs

- Remove your dog's collar before going into the field to prevent the dog being caught up on fences, branches etc

- Know where your dog is at all times when walking up cover

- Know where your dog is when loading and closing a gun, particularly in confined spaces such as a pigeon or duck hide, to avoid accidents

- Check with the keeper if and where you may use your dog to pick up shot game and do not let your dog disturb ground which is still to be shot

- When sending your dog for a retrieve, ensure that other Guns are aware of his location. If in doubt do not send your dog until shooting has ceased. Particular care should be taken when shooting in poor light

- If necessary, and with permission, take your dog over ground previously shot to find any game that was not previously recovered

- Never tie a dog to yourself or your equipment when you are shooting. Use a proper dog anchor if necessary

- Do not send your dog into dangerous situations such as over frozen water or into fast-flowing rivers.

Good training is essential for the field

Following directional hand signals

Steadiness in company is essential   *Training should be enjoyable – for man and dog*

Dogs on the foreshore

- Try to make your dog comfortable – make sure he has a dry seat

- Send your dog to retrieve birds as soon as they are shot

- Do not send your dog into dangerous situations such as fast-flowing currents or onto frozen water

- Dogging the tide line after shooting will often recover lost birds

After shooting

- Check your dog for any injuries, thorns or cuts and treat them promptly. Carry a first aid kit for your dog in the car and in the field

- Ensure your dog has access to water

- Dry your dog off and offer him a light feed before leaving him in the car or driving home

Insurance

- Consider insuring your dog against veterinary fees, accident and illness, accidental death, loss by theft or straying, recovery and legal costs and third party liability. Check that the policy properly covers dogs used for shooting

- Consider marking your dog with a tattoo or implanted chip to help recovery if lost or stolen.

Email: gundogs@basc.org.uk
BASC Gundog hotline: 01823 480 923
for BASC Gundog membership: 01244 573 030

10 – GAMEKEEPING

Anyone involved in game shooting or rough shooting should understand the role of gamekeepers and appreciate the benefits of their work for game shooting, wildlife and habitat management.

THE ROLE OF THE GAMEKEEPER

A gamekeeper, whether professional or amateur, works on a shoot to look after and encourage the game population. He, and sometimes she, may do this by protecting the wild stock and enhancing its breeding potential, by rearing and releasing game birds, and, where necessary, by controlling predators of game. This will augment the overall game population.

Habitat creation and management

It is necessary to create a suitable environment for a healthy game population. The gamekeeper achieves this by working alongside the landowner, farmer or shoot manager to improve and create habitats on the shoot. These provide food, nesting cover and shelter for gamebirds, thus increasing the 'carrying capacity' for game on the shoot.

Gamekeeping and conservation

Good habitat for game also provides good habitat for a whole range of other wildlife, which is a benefit to the countryside. A keepered environment can sustain a greater and more varied wildlife community than one which is unkeepered. The reason for this is that the gamekeeper's work, both in habitat management and also in controlling predators and pests, encourages a great variety of other birds, animals and plants. In this way, the gamekeeper makes a valuable contribution to the conservation of the countryside and to biodiversity.

Supplementing wild game stocks

Wild gamebird populations may need to be supplemented by rearing and releasing additional stocks. On a shoot where there are not sufficient numbers of wild pheasants, partridges or duck to provide a shootable surplus, then it is the gamekeeper's job to rear and release game to supplement the population.

There are four main ways to increase game stocks, and a gamekeeper may use more than one method to source stock for release onto the shoot.

1. Rearing birds from home-produced eggs

Gamebirds are caught and penned towards the end of the shooting season. The following spring these captive birds produce eggs which are incubated and hatched, usually in an incubator. The chicks are then reared by the gamekeeper and released into the wild at six to eight weeks old. The release programme is a gradual process, thus allowing the young birds to acclimatise to their new surroundings.

2. Releasing from purchased eggs to poult stage

The shoot buys gamebird eggs from a game farm. These are incubated; the chicks are reared by the gamekeeper and then released on to the shoot at six to eight weeks old.

3. Releasing from purchased chick to poult stage

Day-old gamebird chicks are bought from a game farm; the chicks are reared and released onto the shoot by the gamekeeper.

4. Releasing bought-in poults

Poults are purchased from a game farm at the age of six to eight weeks and released gradually onto the shoot. The shoot is saved the work of hatching and rearing its own birds, but will pay more for poults than it would for chicks.

BASC recommends that gamekeepers support UK game

Pheasants in rearing pens

farms which rear their birds in traditional and welfare-friendly ways, and check the provenance, health, and well-being of stock in advance of delivery.

Predators

The control of certain ground and avian predators is of utmost importance if gamebirds or ducks are to thrive on a shoot. If these predators are not kept in check, then nesting birds and recently-released poults/ducklings would stand little chance of survival.

The gamekeeper regards as predators those animals which eat eggs, chicks, ducklings, poults and adult birds.

Ground predators

These are ground-dwelling animals which prey on game, especially in the nesting season, and include fox, feral cat, mink, stoat, weasel and brown rat.

Avian predators

All birds of prey are strictly protected by law. However some other species which take the eggs and chicks of game birds and ducks can be controlled under the general licences. This includes carrion crow, hooded crow, rook, jackdaw, magpie, jay, great black-backed gull and lesser black-backed gull.

Methods of predator control

Before carrying out any pest and predator control keepers must ensure they understand and fully comply with all current legislation. Ignorance is no defence. For information on any aspect of pest and predator control contact BASC or check the website www.basc.org.uk

There are five main methods of control available to a gamekeeper:

1. Shooting

The gamekeeper usually carries a shotgun or rifle when working on the shoot and often has the chance to shoot both ground and avian predators. At certain times of the year, shooting foxes at night with a rifle and a powerful lamp is an effective method of control.

2. Trapping – tunnel traps

Artificial tunnels are placed at strategic points round the shoot, each containing a Fenn Mk IV spring trap, or similar. Small ground predators hunting for food will investigate these tunnels and be caught in the trap. Note that only certain spring traps are legal for such use.

3. Trapping – cage traps

Cage traps may be used to catch ground predators and Larsen traps or multi-catchers may be used for avian predators such as magpies, crows and jackdaws. Cage traps may be baited with food and Larsen traps will often contain a live decoy bird, which must have a constant supply of food and water. There are strict requirements under the law for the type and operation of such cage traps.

4. Snaring

The use of free-running snares, set and inspected correctly according to the relevant code of practice, is an efficient way of controlling foxes. No other type of snare is legal.

5. Poison

Poisons are much restricted in their use for pest control but the correct use of legally prescribed poison can be an efficient way of controlling certain pests, such as rats.

Controlling other pests

Very often it is the gamekeeper's job to control other pests which cause damage to agricultural crops or growing timber on the farm or estate. These animals may include rats, rabbits and grey squirrels. Control of these pests may be by shooting or by using legally-approved traps, snares or poison bait. Rabbits may also be flushed into nets with the aid of ferrets.

Magpie in Larsen trap

Shoot day management

The gamekeeper is responsible for the day-to-day management and safe running of the shoot. He works closely with the shoot owner or manager to ensure that the shoot day runs smoothly and his responsibilities will usually include:

1. Guns

Making sure that numbered pegs are correctly positioned for each drive and that suitable transport is available to move the Guns between the drives.

2. Beaters

Organising the transportation and management of beaters during the day.

3. Pickers-up

Ensuring that there are sufficient dog handlers with trained gundogs at each drive, preferably in, but mainly behind, the line of Guns, to retrieve shot and wounded game as quickly as possible.

4. Stops

Making sure that these are strategically and correctly sited at each drive. A 'stop' is someone who is positioned to stop game running or breaking out to the side of the drive.

5. Checking, storage and sale of game

Ensuring that the shot game is collected at the end of each drive. It must be transported, inspected, and stored correctly so that it enters the human food chain in good condition.

6. Checking the ground afterwards

Ensuring that any shot game not previously retrieved is found and collected at the end of the day or early the next morning.

Poaching and trespass

Disturbance of game should be kept to a minimum, not least to make sure it stays on the shoot and is not lost over the boundaries or to unnecessary predation. It is the gamekeeper's job to ensure that this is kept to a minimum. He will be responsible for ensuring that game is not taken by poachers and he will often have a wider responsibility for security around the shoot or estate as a whole.

Well organised beaters are essential on a driven shoot

11 – CARE OF SHOT GAME

Game must always be regarded as food and should be treated as such from the moment it is shot until it reaches the table.

When shooting live quarry always make sure that it is retrieved and that wounded quarry is humanely dispatched as swiftly as possible.

Never intentionally shoot game where it is unlikely to be retrieved, for example over a fast-flowing river or onto land where you do not have permission. If the quarry is to go into the food chain ensure it is free from contamination.

Some species such as crows, foxes and other pests which are not suitable for sale or consumption, should be disposed of in accordance with current legislation. They should not be discarded, left in the countryside or displayed on a gibbet as this can cause offence to other people and serves no justifiable purpose. BASC will be able to advise on current legislation requirements.

Pheasants hanging in game cart

If rearing and releasing game to supplement wild stocks, the aim must be to produce fully mature, healthy and marketable game. In particular red-legged partridges should be at least 15-16 weeks old before shooting commences to ensure this.

It is unacceptable to throw shot quarry into a pile in the back of a truck. This will bruise the meat and prevent the carcasses cooling in the appropriate manner. As a result the quality of the meat will be spoilt, leading to unnecessary wastage of the shot game.

If game is going to be sold, suitable arrangements should be made for its collection, transportation and storage.

All shot game must be handled and stored in a way that is hygienic. It should be stored and transported in a way that allows the heat to disperse as quickly as possible. Where game is to be sold on it might be necessary to install a suitable chiller.

Properly equipped chiller

All shooters must ensure that they comply with relevant game meat and food hygiene regulations.

If surplus game is to be sold to an Approved Game Handling Establishment (AGHE) the law requires that a trained person has inspected the carcasses and holds Lantra's Level 2 Certificate in wild game meat hygiene or an equivalent. The one-day course is available through BASC, and shows how to care for game which is destined to enter the human food chain.

When consuming shot game at home it is recommended that all shot-damaged tissue is removed before cooking to avoid lead contamination and to enhance the attractiveness of the meal.

Well-prepared meals from game birds

All who shoot have a responsibility to care for and make good use of the game which is shot. Respect the animal you have taken.

12 – *SHOOTING AND CONSERVATION*

Introduction

Sporting shooting could not exist without conservation because, if there were no conservation, there would be nothing to shoot. And in preserving habitat for game we benefit a host of other wildlife. Woodland thinned for pheasants, for instance, can contain four times more species of butterfly and ten times as many individual butterflies as unmanaged areas.

In the 21st century the necessity to manage our natural resources becomes ever more pressing. Since Neolithic farmers began to shape the landscape 6,000 years ago man's influence has come to dominate the countryside and even the wildest places are, in essence, a man-made environment. That places a huge responsibility on those who control the countryside. This is not just a UK problem. Increased farming pressure and associated loss of wildlife, or biodiversity, as it is more often known, is happening around the globe.

In response to these global losses, the Convention on Biological Diversity (CBD) was agreed in 1992 at the United Nations' Conference on Environment and Development in Rio de Janeiro – usually known as the Earth Summit.

The UK was one of 150 countries signing the convention, committing them to provide a plan for the conservation and sustainable use of biodiversity. Consequently the UK Biodiversity Action Plan (UKBAP) was produced in 1994 and it is this which sets targets for the conservation and sustainable use of the UK's threatened wildlife.

Since 1994 it has become increasingly clear that conservationists must think on the large scale. Isolated nature reserves, offering little pools of shelter, are not the answer; the two key concepts are 'landscape scale' and 'connectivity.'

In essence this means conserving habitat over a wide area where the individual woods or other features are linked by wildlife corridors such as hedgerows or overgrown streams. This approach has become increasingly important to provide wildlife with the flexibility it requires to adapt to climate change. Shooting is one of the few activities which directly influences land management on this scale; it therefore has a crucial role in helping the UK achieve its internationally-agreed conservation targets.

Shooters now find themselves in a unique situation because of the management they do. With increasing financial and institutional pressure on farmers to manage their land for enhanced biodiversity, shooting offers exceptional opportunities. By improving habitat landowners can simultaneously increase their income from shooting rents and reap the financial benefits of environmental stewardship schemes.

With over two thirds of the rural land area shot over, and shooting spending over £250 million on conservation each year, shooting sports are key partners for biodiversity conservation. At the heart of this is the BASC Green Shoots programme – a biodiversity action plan for shooting launched in 2000 'to recognise, build upon and co-ordinate the shooting community's considerable contribution to wildlife and biodiversity conservation'.

Since its launch Green Shoots has demonstrated how the shooting community can enhance biodiversity on privately held land where the statutory conservation agencies and non-governmental organisations face their greatest challenge in accessing and influencing management for biodiversity. It is fair to say that without this active participation of the shooting community the UK is unlikely to achieve the conservation targets to which the government is committed. Shooters spend 2.7 million work days on conservation – the equivalent of 12,000 full-time jobs.

However, these projects are not run in isolation. BASC believes in working with others, and all our projects benefit from strong partnerships with the public, private and voluntary sectors.

It is against this background that shooters have to carry out their conservation work, and it is crucial for the future of shooting sports that those who shoot have a basic knowledge of issues relating to the countryside and its wildlife.

Geology and topography

The rocks that make up the United Kingdom not only create our landscape but they also influence the soils and with that the plants and animals that will exist there. Within the United Kingdom you will find nearly all the rock types and landscape features found in much larger countries. Our mountains may not be the highest and our rivers are not the longest, but it is difficult to travel many miles without crossing a geological boundary and with it a change in landscape. The gently rolling lowland areas with their hidden rocks produce landscapes including chalk downland, arable plains, the once-wet fenland areas of Cambridgeshire and sandy heaths like those in Dorset or the Breckland of Norfolk. These areas contrast with the rugged, glacier-gouged rocks of western Scotland and Snowdonia. The plants and animals that can be found on different rocks and soils are also influenced by temperature. Temperature generally drops the further north you go or the higher you go.

Conservation concepts

Conservation does not mean neglect. Some people see conservation as leaving nature to look after itself; this is not the case and will inevitably lead to a change in how the site looks and its value for wildlife. Conservation on a shoot involves making choices. There will always be limits to what can be done, driven by cost, practicality and personal interest. The first stage is to draw up a plan.

Flight ponds are havens for wildlife

Habitat

Habitat is the environment that supplies everything wildlife needs to sustain healthy populations. Different wildlife species require particular habitats. Habitats are classified into broadly distinctive types according to their location, flora and fauna, physical characteristics and geology, i.e. lowland deciduous woodland or heathland. Each habitat type provides the food, cover, water and space for the wildlife living there.

Conservation plan

Identify which are the most important habitats on the shoot. Are any of the habitats important at the national, regional or local level? Recognise habitats that cannot be influenced – arable fields, grass leys. Identify key boundaries which might act as corridors for wildlife. Write a plan to cover management of all appropriate habitats.

Habitat management

The foundation stone of wildlife management is the provision of suitable habitats. In the UK man has changed the face of nature through agriculture and hunting for thousands of years so that much of the wildlife we enjoy today is a result of man's intervention.

Aspects of the habitat that can be managed are the availability of food and water and the provision of cover or open spaces. Countryside which provides a mixture of habitats is clearly desirable since it can support a greater variety of species. It is also important to bear in mind that each wildlife species occupies a unique place in the environment. If a particular habitat changes in character or is altered by management some species may do well and others decline. Inappropriate management of a woodland habitat for pheasants or ponds for mallards, for example, can have a negative effect on other species.

Species management

Some wildlife can harm other species and their habitat if not controlled. This is particularly true of non-native species which are now adapted to the British countryside and can harm native plants and animals. Where populations get too large or individuals cause specific problems, nature reserve managers and game managers have to act to maintain balance.

Examples of where control may be necessary include: populations of deer which have grown to the extent that they are severely damaging habitat; magpies and crows that prey on game and songbird chicks and eggs; and the non-native mink that can severely reduce wildfowl and water vole populations.

The intention is always to maintain a balance rather than to eradicate any species.

Communities

A community in this context is a group of plants or animals existing in a habitat, usually dependent in some way on one another for survival. Only by maintaining entire communities is it likely that the complex and the interdependent needs of different species can be satisfied.

Succession

Left alone, nature changes habitats through a process called 'succession'. As a lake fills with silt it gradually becomes a pond, then a marsh and beyond this dry land and a forest. Similarly, moorland left to nature would become covered in scrub and eventually revert to woodland.

Many of the most important wildlife communities in the UK are at an early successional stage and much effort of conservationists is taken up in suspending successional changes e.g. coppicing woodland, in order to maximise the benefits of these early successional stages.

Water voles are helped by mink control

Competition

Plants and animals compete for the same resources, usually food or space. The diversity of a particular habitat and its species is often affected by competition for the same food resource by the species present. An example of competition is that between red squirrels and grey squirrels. Grey squirrels feed on unripe hazel nuts and acorns and therefore harvest the hazel nuts before they are ready for red squirrels that prefer the ripened nuts. This leads to reduced feeding opportunities for red squirrels, causing them, depending on other factors, to decline.

In this case therefore habitat management would involve improving conditions for the more vulnerable species, i.e. the red squirrel. This could be done by, for example, not planting oak trees, on whose acorns grey squirrels thrive, in areas where grey squirrels are present.

Predation

Predation can be defined as one animal being 'preyed upon' or acting as a food resource, for another. For example, hedgehogs, which are preyed upon by badgers are only common in areas where badgers are scarce, such as urban settlements where badger predation is low. It has been shown that by reducing dominant predator species the surrounding communities can benefit from an increase in diversity. In game managment it has been shown that by reducing the numbers of predatory species, such as corvids (crows, magpies etc.), game managers increase the diversity of woodland species such as song birds.

Management and monitoring

Monitoring is an important part of any programme of habitat management, to ensure that work carried out has the desired outcome.

MODERN CONSERVATION

The national blueprint for conservation is the UKBAP which, as explained, was initiated after the Rio Earth Summit. It is overseen in each of the UK nations by a statutory authority; these are Natural England, the Countryside Council for Wales, Scottish Natural Heritage and Environment and Heritage Northern Ireland.

Beneath these government agencies is a huge variety of NGOs. These include national organisations, such as the RSPB, county wildlife trusts, local conservation groups, shooting syndicates and wildfowling clubs, all contributing at various levels. But all their efforts are directed by the UKBAP; this was produced by a steering group which identified key species and habitats that were thought to be most at risk, and separate strategies were devised for each one. Within this wider framework Local Biodiversity Action Plans (LBAPs) were developed to reflect the local needs of wildlife and its habitat. This is where the shooting community makes a vital contribution.

Shooting as an incentive for conservation

Shooting provides a powerful incentive for the conservation of habitats, for example through the creation of ponds or coppicing of woodland. But although this may provide financial returns, it is not simply a matter of money. Enjoyable sport in a self-managed and wildlife-rich landscape is often the only return sought by those who shoot.

Nevertheless the data provided by the independent PACEC study in 2006 shows that the value of conservation work undertaken by the shooting community is impressive:

- Shooting is involved in the management of an area the size of Scotland
- Two million hectares are actively managed for conservation as a result of shooting
- Shoot providers spend £250 million a year on conservation
- Shooters spend 2.7 million work days a year on conservation – the equivalent of 12,000 full-time jobs.

APPENDIX 1

THE BRITISH ASSOCIATION FOR SHOOTING AND CONSERVATION

The British Association for Shooting and Conservation is the UK's largest shooting organisation, supported by over 130,000 members. BASC represents and safeguards the interests of all who enjoy shooting sports.

BASC has five prime objectives. These are to ensure that owners of sporting firearms have:

The British Association for Shooting and Conservation

- A strong and unified voice for shooting
- All-party backing for shooting
- Balanced comment in the media
- Continuing opportunity to go shooting
- High standards

The association has eight country and regional centres and a headquarters at Rossett, near Wrexham.

BASC has the UK's only full-time firearms team, offering help and advice on all firearms matters and protecting the lawful right to use sporting firearms. It also has dedicated teams covering gamekeeping, conservation, research, training, deer, wildfowling, political and public affairs.

The association has forged links with MPs of all parties to ensure the voice of responsible shooting is heard in the political arena. It is responsible for all three major parties including commitments to responsible shooting in their manifestos.

Most importantly BASC promotes the belief and practice that shooting and conservation go hand-in-hand. The Government now recognises this fact, and quoted BASC in its white paper on rural affairs. BASC's Green Shoots programme creates partnerships with other conservation organisations at all levels and people are increasingly aware that shooters represent a massive army of conservationists who get out into the field, and by their own efforts make our countryside a better place for wildlife.

Courses
A wide variety of introductory days and practical courses is run by BASC covering most aspects of shooting. Many of these are tailored specifically to the needs of particular groups, such as young people or women. They are not exclusively for members and you can find details on the BASC website or by contacting the shooting standards department on 01244 573018 or email shootingstandards@basc.org.uk

Contact BASC
Phone: 01244 573000 - **Fax:** 01244 573001 - **Email:** enq@basc.org.uk - **Website:** www.basc.org.uk
Postal address: Marford Mill, Rossett, Wrexham, LL12 0HL

Advice
Free advice is available to all BASC members at the end of a phone, or email:

Firearms	01244 573010	firearms@basc.org.uk
Game and gamekeeping	01244 573019	gamekeeping@basc.org.uk
Conservation & land management	01244 573024	conservation@basc.org.uk
Deer	01244 573047	deer@basc.org.uk
Wildfowling	01244 573011	wildfowling@basc.org.uk
Press office	01244 573031	pressoff@basc.org.uk
Gundog helpline	01823 480923	gundogs@basc.org.uk
Research	01244 573016	research@basc.org.uk
Shooting standards	01244 573018	shootingstandards@basc.org.uk

APPENDIX 2

CODES OF PRACTICE

The Code of Good Shooting Practice has been agreed by all the major shooting organisations and provides a comprehensive guide to responsible game shooting. Everyone who shoots game should be familiar with it.

Additionally BASC issues codes of practice covering individual aspects of shooting sports. These are frequently up-dated and are supplemented by advice notes. They are obtainable free from BASC head office or can be downloaded from the BASC website. Those currently available include:

The Code of Good Shooting Practice
Air rifles
Deer stalking
Disruption of shoots by demonstrators
Flight ponds
Fox snaring
Gundogs
Horses and shoots
Lamping
Picking-up
Respect for quarry
Shotgun safety
Transport of beaters
Trapping pest birds
Trapping pest mammals
Use of a dog below ground (England and Wales)
Wildfowling
Woodpigeon shooting

APPENDIX 3

WILDLIFE LAW

The Joint Nature Conservation Committee, which is a statutory adviser to the Government gives a full explanation of the Wildlife and Countryside Act 1981, and subsequent amendments, on its website. There is also a fully downloadable copy of the Act. You will find this at www.jncc.gov.uk

The general licences which allow pest shooting can be found, with explanatory notes, on the websites of Natural England, Scottish Natural Heritage, Countryside Council for Wales and Northern Ireland Environment Agency.

To the best of our knowledge the legal information given in this book is correct at the time of going to press. However there are occasionally changes to the law and the general licences are subject to annual review. For the most up-to-date information visit the BASC website. If you are a member advice is freely available by phone or e-mail.

APPENDIX 4

SHOOTING TECHNIQUE

LEAD OR FORWARD ALLOWANCE

A shotgun is designed to give the shooter an advantage when bringing down moving quarry, whether it is running or flying. Consequently shotguns are pointed, not aimed.

Humans are capable of great accuracy and, with a gun that fits, any shooter can point the muzzle where they want the shot to be; the art of shooting is ensuring that that point coincides with the target. This means that successful shotgun shooting is founded on the basic understanding that to hit a moving target requires a moving gun.

The shooter must accept the fact that to hit a moving target the pellets must be thrown ahead of it. Forward allowance or lead must therefore be understood and, for many targets, actually seen.

Lead or forward allowance and the amount each target needs can only be taught by visual representation and actual shooting. Each person must develop their own barrel-to-target relationship 'picture' for a successful shot.

THE TECHNIQUES

There are three basic ways of obtaining the necessary picture. All three have the same conclusion. It is only the system of picking up the speed and direction of the target which varies.

Any 'patent method' of shooting a moving target will be found to be based on one of these techniques.

TECHNIQUE 1 – The Method

This is the most trouble-free technique for teaching the basics of shotgun shooting.

- The target is picked up by pointing the muzzles of the mounted gun at the target, at the point where it is clearly visible on its trajectory, and the gun moved smoothly with it
- After establishing the speed and direction, with the gun in the shoulder, the muzzles are moved ahead of the target to establish the correct sight picture of forward allowance or lead
- The trigger is pulled once the correct lead is established and the gun continues along the target's trajectory
- The target breaks.

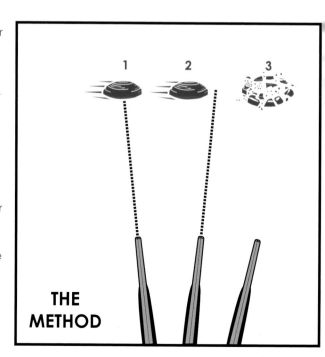

THE METHOD

TECHNIQUE 2 – Smoke Trail

The only difference between the Smoke Trail technique and The Method is the manner in which the trajectory and the speed of the target are established.

As the name implies, Smoke Trail means the muzzles of the mounted gun are brought from behind the target (along its smoke trail), then with it, and so ahead and following through after the shot as with The Method.

This technique can be useful in creating and maintaining the necessary swing and follow through. It is often the technique naturally employed by those who mainly shoot driven pheasants and has been taught as 'bum – belly – beak – bang!'

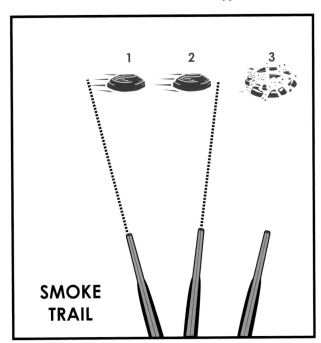

SMOKE TRAIL

TECHNIQUE 3 – Maintained Lead

Again this is a self-explanatory title. In this case the necessary lead is established virtually immediately the target is picked up.

Muzzles and target move at the same speed and in the same direction. The sight picture is established, the trigger is pulled and the gun movement continues just as with the other two techniques.

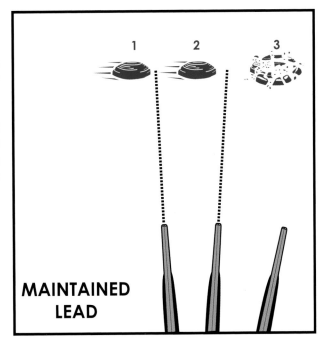

MAINTAINED LEAD

REMEMBER
- Moving target – moving gun
- Pick up, picture and follow through are fluid actions
- All three techniques of obtaining lead are momentary actions
- Establish the correct picture or muzzle/target relationship in your mind

APPENDIX 5
RECOMMENDED FURTHER READING

There is a considerable number of shooting books on the market covering all aspects of the sport. The three principal publishers of shooting books are: **Quiller** and **Swan Hill Press** at www.countrybooksdirect.com **Merlin Unwin** at www.merlinunwin.co.uk and **Crowood Press** at www.crowoodpress.co.uk

The following list of recommended books is intended to take you beyond the basic principles laid out in this volume

Shooting

The BASC Guide to Shooting Game by Michael Yardley. Swan Hill Press. ISBN 978 1904057970

The Game Shooting Handbook by Mike Barnes. Crowood Press. ISBN 1861268041

Wildfowling – a BASC Handbook. Edited by Jeffrey Olstead. Quiller. ISBN 978 1846890253

The Pigeon Shooter by John Batley. Swan Hill Press. ISBN 978 1840371253

Rough Shooting by Mike Swan. Swan Hill Press. ISBN 978 1846890109

Law
Fair Game – the law of country sports by Charlie Parkes and John Thornley. Pelham Books. ISBN 07207 20656

Firearms
The Sporting Shotgun by Robin Marshall-Ball. Swan Hill Press. ISBN 978 1904057086

The Shotgun Handbook by Mike George. Crowood Press. ISBN 978 1861261571

Conservation
Management Planning for Nature Conservation edited by Mike Alexander. Springer-Verlag. ISBN 978 1402065804

Habitat Management for Conservation: A Handbook of Techniques by Malcolm Ausden. Oxford University Press. ISBN 978 0198568735

Woodland Management For Birds : A Guide to Managing for Declining Woodland Birds in England by N Symes and F Currie. RSPB. ISBN 1901930564

Habitat Management for Invertebrates by P Kirkby. RSPB/JNCC ISBN 1901930300

A Management Guide to Birds of Lowland and Farmland by R Winspear and G Davies. RSPB. ISBN 1901930572

Field guides
Collins Bird Guide (Paperback) by Lars Svensson, Killian Mullarney, Dan Zetterstrom and Peter J Grant. HarperCollins. ISBN 0007113323

RSPB Complete Birds of Britain & Europe – 70 minute audio CD by R. Hume. Dorling. ISBN 978 1405322287

Field guide to the mammals of Britain and Europe by David W McDonald and Priscilla Barret. Collins. ISBN 002197790

INDEX

Approved Game Handling Establishments (AGHEs) 130

badger 47, 134
barnacle goose 73
barrels
 bores 18–19
 choke 16, 19–20, 106
 cleaning 23
 construction 12
 Damascus 27
 obstruction 37, 39
 ribs 14, 32
 wear and damage 32, 33
bats 47
bean goose 70
behaviour in the field see codes of conduct
bismuth shot 26, 106, 111
black grouse 60, 83, 102
blue hare see mountain hare
boats, wildfowling and 114
bolt-action shotguns 15
bores 18–19
boxlock action 14
breech 17
brent goose 73
bridle ways, shooting from 44
British Association for Shooting and Conservation 8, 10, 11, 107, 136
 codes of practice 28, 137
 courses 136
 education and training 10, 136
 Green Shoots programme 131–2
 gundog training days 121
 insurance package 40
 proficiency award scheme (PAS) 10
 Wildfowling Permit Scheme 107
brown hare 61, 91

Canada goose, habits 58, 73
carrion crow 61, 86, 126
cartridges 24–7
 cartridge mixing 40
 case 24
 components 24–5
 driven game 106
 length 24, 26
 load 26
 roughshooting 97
 safety 24, 32–3, 40
 shot sizes 26, 27
 and shotgun patterning 29
 storage 24, 33
 wildfowling 111–12
chambers 17
choke 16, 19–20, 106
 degrees of choke 19
 effect of 20

fixed-choke 20
multi-choke 20
chough 86
cleaning see maintenance, shotgun
clothing 52, 103, 114
coastal shooting 107–9
 see also wildfowling
codes of conduct 28
 behaviour in the field 51–4
 Code of Good Shooting Practice 103, 137
 driven shooting 103–6
 roughshooting 97–100
 wildfowling 110–16
conservation 131–5
 BASC Green Shoots programme 131–2
 gamekeepers and 125
 habitat management 125, 133, 134
 predator control 134
 shooting as incentive for 135
 species management 133
 UK Biodiversity Action Plan (UKBAP) 131, 135
coot 46, 47, 59, 75
corvids, identification 60, 86–90
crows see carrion crow; corvids; hooded crow

dabbling ducks 57, 61–6
decoys
 live animals 47, 48
 pigeon shooting 96
deer stalking 50
diving ducks 58, 67–9
double-barrelled shotguns 12, 16
driven game shooting 101–6
 safety 105
 shooting etiquette 103–6
drop-down action shotguns 15
ducks 46, 108
 coastal shooting 107–16
 identification 57–8, 61–9
 inland duck shooting 95

education and training 10, 136
ejectors 15
European Firearms Pass (EFP) 42

ferreting 96, 127
flight lining 96
footpaths, shooting from 44
fore-end 18, 22
.410 shotguns 18
foxes 127
free shooting 50

gadwall 57, 66
Game Acts 50, 101, 102
game licences 50

gamebirds
 definition 101
 driven 101–6
 identification 59–60, 79–84
 increasing stock of 125–6
 open and close seasons 102
 roughshooting 95
gamekeeping 125–8
 and conservation 125
 habitat management 125
 increasing game stocks 125–6
 pest and predator control 126–7
shoot day management 128
garganey 62
geese 27, 46, 108
 coastal shooting 107–16
 identification 58, 70–3
general licences 45, 48, 137
golden plover 46, 47, 59, 76, 108
goldeneye 58, 69
grey partridge 59, 80
grey plover 76
grey squirrel 94, 134
greylag goose 58, 70
grouse 27, 102
 see also black Grouse; red grouse
gulls 56, 126
gun fit 21
gundogs 117–24
 acquiring 120
 breeds 117–21
 care of 106, 115, 116, 122, 124
 in cars 122
 control of 36, 52
 handling in the field 121, 123
 insurance 124
 roughshooting 96, 106
 safety 123
 training 120–1
 wildfowling 115–16, 124

habitat 56, 133
 management 125, 133, 134
hammerless guns 14
hare 27, 50
 identification 60, 91–2
 killing by hand 54
highways, shooting on or near 44
hooded crow 61, 86, 126
hunt-point-retrieve (HPR) breeds 119–20

insurance 40, 104
 gundogs 124

jack snipe 77, 102
jackdaw 60, 88, 126
jay 60, 90, 126

lapwing 76
law 41–50, 137
 land ownership 50
 nightshooting 44
 open seasons 44, 45
 police powers 43–4
 possession of shotguns by young people 43
 shotguns in public places 44
 see also shotgun certificates
lead shot restrictions 26, 46, 103, 111
levers 16
licences see game licences; general licences
loading shutguns 36
loss or theft of shotguns 34

magpie 60, 89, 126
maintenance, shotgun 22–3, 34
 after wildfowling 116
 annual service 23, 32
mallard 27, 47, 57, 63, 109
master eye 21
misfires 36, 37
moorhen 46, 47, 59, 74
mountain (blue) hare 60, 92

National Proficiency Tests Council (NPTC) 10
nightshooting, law and 44, 50
non-lead shot 26, 27
Northern Ireland
 firearms certificates 42, 43
 identification of foreshore 107
 lead shot restrictions 111
 open seasons 49, 102
 quarry species 48–9
 sale of dead wild birds 49
 young people and shotguns 43

open seasons 44, 45, 102
 quarry species 45
over-under shotguns 12, 14, 15, 18
 choke 20
 triggers 16
overshooting 54, 99

partridges 27, 102
 see also grey partridge; red-legged partridge
pattern, patterning 20, 27, 29, 112
pegs 104, 128
pest and predators 56
 control of 126–7, 134
 disposal of dead pests 129
 and general licences 45
 identification 60
 shooting 53, 98, 104

pheasant 27, 79
  identification 59, 79
  open season 79, 102
pigeons
  identification 60, 85
  racing 46
  see also woodpigeon
pink-footed goose 58, 71, 108
pintail 47, 57, 64
poaching 128
pochard 47, 58, 68
pointers 119
poison, for vermin control 127
police and shooting law 41, 42, 43–4, 44
Principles of Live Quarry Shooting (PLQS) course 10, 11
prohibited killing methods 48
proof marks 32–3
  unproved guns 33
protected animals 45, 46, 47
ptarmigan 60, 84, 102
public places, shotguns in 44
public rights of way 51
pump-action shotguns 15
  safety 17, 31

quail 81
quarry identification 55–101
  basic principles 55–6
  categories 57–60
  field guides 55
  individual species 61–94

rabbit
  ferreting 96, 127
  identification 60, 93
  killing by hand 54
  shooting 50, 96
racing pigeons 46
range, shotgun 27, 28, 53
  shooting within 53, 98
  wildfowling 113
rats 127
raven 86, 88
red grouse 60, 82, 102
red squirrel 47, 134
red-breasted merganser 63
red-legged partridge 59, 81, 129
removing a gun from its slip 35
replacing a gun in its slip 35
retrievers 117–18
ribs 14, 32
roads, shooting on or near 44
rock dove 85
rook 60, 86, 126
roost shooting 96
roughshooting 95–100
  code of conduct 97–100
  for game 95
  inland duck shooting 95
  safety 98

safety 30–40
  arc of fire 37
  carrying shotguns 35, 36

cartridges 24, 32–3, 40
children and guns 33
closing a shotgun 35
condition of gun 31–2
crossing obstacles 38–9
driven game shooting 105
in the field 35–40
gundogs 123
handling shotguns 30–3, 35–9, 105
in the home 33–4
insurance 40, 104
law and 44–5
loading 36
misfires 36, 37
proof marks 32–3
roughshooting 98
while travelling 34
wildfowling 113
safety catches 17, 36
sale of surplus game 47, 130
scaup 67, 68
Scotland
  foreshore, definition of 108
  lead shot restrictions 46
security 33
semi-automatic shotguns 13, 15, 17
  gas operated 13
  recoil operated 13
  restrictions on use 48, 111
  safety 31
  safety catches 17
setters 119
shoot management 125–8
shooting rights 101
shooting technique 138–9
  lead or forward allowance 138
  Maintained Lead technique 139
  The Method 138
  Smoke Trail technique 139
shot sizes 26, 27, 106, 112
shotgun certificates 13, 26, 41–2, 51
  conditions of issue 41
  European Firearms Pass (EFP) 42
  Northern Ireland 42, 43
  prohibited persons 41
  refusal/revocation of 44
shotguns 12–23
  bolt action 15
  boxlock action 14
  buying or selling 41, 42
  construction 12
  definition 12
  double-barrelled 12, 16
  drop-down action 15
  hammerless 14
  handling 30–3
  loss or theft of 34
  maintenance 22–3
  over-under 12, 14, 15, 16, 18, 20
  pump-action 15, 17, 31

range 27, 28, 53
self-loaders 13, 15
semi-automatic 13, 15, 17, 48, 111
side-by-side 12, 14
sidelock action 14
single-barrelled 13
storage 33
three-barrelled 13
wear and damage 31–2
see also individual parts
shoveler 47, 57, 65
side-by-side shotguns 14, 15, 18
  choke 20
  triggers 16
sidelock action 14
16-bore shotguns 19
snares, for vermin control 127
snipe 27, 47, 77
  identification 59, 77
  open season 46, 77, 102
  roughshooting 95
spaniels 118
squirrels 27, 60, 94
  see also grey squirrel; red squirrel
steel shot 25, 26, 111, 112
stock 15–16, 21
  cast of 15
  cleaning 22
  height 21
  shapes 16
  wear and damage 32
stock dove 85
'stops' and pickers-up 104, 128
storage
  of cartridges 33
  of game 100, 128, 129–30
  of shotguns 33
Sundays
  shooting game on 44, 46
  wildfowling on 110

teal 27, 47, 62
  coastal shooting 109
  identification 57, 62
10-bore shotguns 19
28-bore shotguns 19
top levers 16
trapping vermin 127
trespass 44, 50, 98
triggers 16
tufted duck 47, 58, 67
tungsten-based shot 26, 111, 112
12-bore shotguns 17, 18, 19
20-bore shotguns 18, 19

unsporting behaviour 98

vermin see pest and predators

waders
  coastal shooting 108
  habits 108
  identification 59, 76–8
white-fronted goose 58, 72

wigeon 47, 58, 61, 109
wildfowl
  habits 108
  identification 57–9, 61–73
  rough shoots 95
wildfowling 107–16
  equipment 114
  foreshore, definition 107–8
  gundogs 115–16, 124
  guns and cartridges 111–13
  principles 110–16
  rough shooting 95
  safety 113
  shooting from a boat 114
  on Sundays 110
Wildfowling Permit Scheme 107
Wildlife and Countryside Act 1981 45–8, 109, 137
  open seasons 45, 46, 102
  prohibited killing methods 48
  sale of dead birds 47
woodcock 47, 78
  identification 59, 78
  open season 46, 78, 102
woodpigeon 27, 47, 85
  decoying 96
  flight lining 96
  identification 60, 85
  roost shooting 196
  shooting 96
wounded quarry, retrieving and dispatching 54, 97, 105, 129

young people
  gun handling 33
  gun safety 33
  possession of shotguns 43